F

Who Can It Be Now?

The Lyrics Game That Takes You Back to the '80s . . . One Line at a Time

Peter T. Fornatale
and Frank R. Scatoni

Fireside
Published by
Simon + Schuster

FIRESIDE
Rockefeller Center
1230 Avenue of the Americas
New York, NY 10020

F

Manufactured in the United States of America

1   3   5   7   9   10   8   6   4   2

Library of Congress
Cataloging-in-Publication Data
Fornatale, Peter.
Who can it be now?: the lyrics game that takes
you back to the '80s—one line at a time /
Peter T. Fornatale and Frank R. Scatoni.
p. cm.
1. Music—Miscellanea. 2. Questions and
answers. 3. Popular music—1981–1990—Texts.
4. Rock music—1981–1990—Texts.
I. Scatoni, Frank R., date. II. Title.
ML63.F45 1998
782.42164'0268—dc21   98-30732   CIP MN
ISBN 0-684-85630-1

Design ▶▶
Sam Potts

Photo Credits

All photos not credited below are
courtesy of Photofest.
Photo on page 3 courtesy of
Kate Marlowe.
Photos on pages 15, 16, 22, 38, 52, 58,
126, 140 (top), 150, and 198 courtesy of
AP/Wide World Photos.
Rubik's Cube, page 76, courtesy of
Kim Marie Scatoni.

To the dearly departed:

Eddie Rabbitt,

Rob Pilatus,

Michael Hutchence,

and Falco

This is your
brain . . .

This is your brain on the '80s Lyrics Game.

How much of your brain is wasted on memorized song lyrics?

You're about to find out.

You're in a bar and some guy comes up to you and says, "Suckin' on a chili dog outside the Tastee Freez." Your first reaction is to sock him in the jaw. But you start to think . . . it isn't some perverse pick-up line. It's a lyric from a song . . . and you know it. Everybody knows it. It's "Jack and Diane" by John Cougar Mellencamp or whatever he was calling himself back in 1982.

Your answer is met with a nod of approval, so he hits you with another one: "I've seen a million faces and I've rocked them all." You think for a second . . . the melody slowly creeps into your head . . . you start to sing out loud . . . "Wanted Dead or Alive." And it all comes back to you—the song, the album, Jon Bon Jovi's hair.

Congratulations, you've just become the latest victim of the '80s Lyrics Game. Welcome to dinner conversation for the next eight weeks.

In *Who Can It Be Now?* we've taken over five hundred '80s lyrics ranging from the sublime ("I said to my reflection, 'Let's get out of this place'") to the ridiculous ("You make the sun shine brighter than Doris Day"), from the sacred ("No saints, no sinners, no devil as well") to the profane (insert your favorite Prince lyric here). Your task: to give the song and the artist for every lyric we throw at you.

In addition to the lyrics and answers, we've included an eclectic assortment of bizarre facts, useless trivia, and silly jokes about the artists who made the '80s such a . . . shall we say, "unique" decade for music.

So whether you still cherish your autographed copy of *Rio* or twitch uncontrollably every time someone plays "99 Luftballons" at a party, you're sure to find the '80s Lyrics Game addictive. Don't believe us? Wait until you start playing.

Introduction

"I was working as a waitress in a cocktail bar"

If you haven't heard this lyric, either you slept through 1982 or you're deaf. **"Don't You Want Me"** by **the Human League** was (and still is) one of the most memorable songs of the decade. The only thing bigger in July of that year was Steven Spielberg's *E.T. The Extra-Terrestrial*, which went on to gross $400 million. Legend has it that E.T.'s face was modeled after Albert Einstein and Carl Sandburg. In retrospect, he looked more like a cross between Yoda and Clara "Where's the beef?" Peller.

"Just a man and his will to survive"

Who would have ever guessed that a rockhead like Sylvester Stallone could make a movie as good as *Rocky* or one as successful as *Rambo*? The lyric is from **Survivor's "Eye of the Tiger,"** the theme song of *Rocky III*, which costarred the former bodyguard with the badass mohawk, Mr. T, as Clubber Lang. T's other '80s achievements included a starring role in *The A-Team*, a brief stint as a professional wrestler, a rap album, and an autobiography (and yes, he really did write it!). He was so successful, they even made a Mr. T doll. We pity the fool who bought it.

Here's T starring in the abominable comedy D.C. Cab.

Prince

(or whatever he's calling himself this week)

Everyone knows these four things about Prince: he was born Prince Rogers Nelson; he hails from Minneapolis, Minnesota; he adores the color purple; and he's about four feet tall. There's no denying his incredible musical talent, but you gotta feel bad for the guy: All of his girlfriends are taller than him. Here's a guy winning Grammys left and right, when—let's face it—he would have looked more at home on the back of Swale in the Belmont Stakes Post Parade.

1. "When I saw all the pictures of the jockeys that were there before me"

2. "And if the elevator tries to bring you down"

3. "Dig if you will the picture"

4. "Seems that I was busy doing something close to nothing"

5. "You don't have to watch *Dynasty* to have an attitude"

6. "The sky was all purple"

7. "I met her in a hotel lobby masturbating with a magazine"

8. "Hurricane Annie ripped the ceiling off a church"

9. "I only wanted to one time see you laughing"

10. "I'm your messiah and you're the reason why"

Okay, okay, we'll call you whatever you want, just put your shirt back on.

1. "Little Red Corvette"
2. "Let's Go Crazy"
3. "When Doves Cry"
4. "Raspberry Beret"
5. "Kiss"
6. "1999"
7. "Darling Nikki"
8. "Sign 'O' the Times"
9. "Purple Rain"
10. "I Would Die 4 U"

Throughout his career Prince was linked romantically or otherwise to a handful of female artists (not to mention Kim Basinger). Can you name the Prince song and the Prince chick?

Purple Harem

1. "She doesn't need a man's touch"

2. "I'm lookin' for a man that'll do it anywhere"

3. "Come on kiss the gun"

4. "I was kissin' Valentino by a crystal blue Italian stream"

5. "Lemme take you somewhere you've never been"

Bonus points if you can guess their height.
Just kidding.

1. **"The Glamorous Life"** by Sheila E.
2. **"Nasty Girl"** by Vanity 6
3. **"Sex Shooter"** by Apollonia 6
4. **"Manic Monday"** by the Bangles
5. **"Sugar Walls"** by Sheena Easton

Sheila Escovedo, aka Sheila E.

"Everyone's a Captain Kirk"

Okay, so we cheated here. Who knows what the real line is,* but we thought the German version would be a little too obvious. Actually, "99 Red Balloons" was the flip side English version of **Nena's** international hit, **"99 Luftballons,"** a song about some kid's balloon starting a nuclear war. Nena's moment in the sun had ended by the time a nasty rumor circulated around grade schools across America that she had died of a drug overdose.

* The real line is: *"Hielten sich für Captain Kirk"*

"I ain't the worst that you've seen"

Sorry, David Lee Roth, but fifteen years later, you're pretty close. What did you do with all that spandex? And can you still do one of those flying kicks without pulling your groin? But back in the day, David Lee really rocked the house. Within a year of **Van Halen's "Jump,"** Roth would be off doing his own thing, while the band played on with new lead singer Sammy Hagar, perhaps the only front man at the time with more hair than Roth himself.

Do you remember the kid in class with the Goody hairbrush in the back pocket of his mangy jeans, the long, feathered hair, the three-quarter-sleeve Metallica shirt, the air-brushed cover-art denim jacket, the leather wallet with the metal chain? Well, this is what he was listening to during the '80s. (Our condolences if this is what you were listening to, too.)

1. "Girls rock your boys"

2. "I scream my heart out, just to make a dime"

3. "So what is wrong with another sin?"

4. "At the drive-in, in the old man's Ford"

5. "If that's your best, your best won't do"

6. "I'm hot, sticky sweet, from my head to my feet"

7. "Enslaving the young and destroying the old"

8. "Don't wanna wait 'til you know me better"

9. "Like a drifter I was born to walk alone"

10. "If you got the money, honey, we got your disease"

Cheeze Metal Jamboree

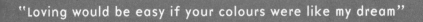

"Loving would be easy if your colours were like my dream"

Do you remember the video for **"Karma Chameleon"** by **Culture Club?** Boy George looked ridiculous. With Bo Derek braids and a makeup job worthy of Bozo, George was like a wreck on the highway—America couldn't look away. George's high-profile popularity even led to a reference in the Arnold Schwarzenegger movie *Commando*. (Read in thick Austrian accent): "Why don't they call him Girl George and cut down on the confusion?"

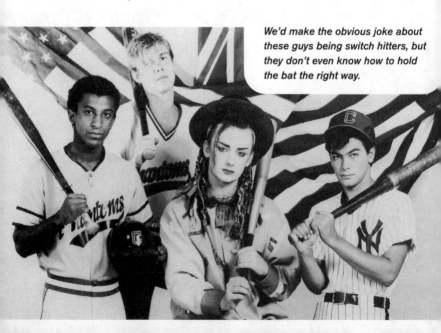

We'd make the obvious joke about these guys being switch hitters, but they don't even know how to hold the bat the right way.

What do the Cars, the Cure, and Haircut 100 have in common? At one point in each of their careers, they were all labeled "New Wave." "New Wave" was essentially a meaningless term used by fans and critics to describe any record that came out in the early '80s that didn't sound like Michael Jackson.

1. "Show me, show me, show me how you do that trick"
2. "I used to think that the day would never come"
3. "Sometimes you're better off dead"
4. "I'm so in love with you, I'll be forever blue"
5. "If I, I get to know your name"
6. "Where does it go from here?"
7. "Making love to you was never second best"
8. "Hit me with your laser beam"
9. "I'm a one-night stand"
10. "Moving through the doorway of a nation"
11. "Sometimes I feel I've got to run away"
12. "There's something about you, girl, that makes me sweat"
13. "You and I should get along so awfully"
14. "I am human and I need to be loved"
15. "She floats like a swan, grace on the water"

Mope Rock, New Wave, and Other "Alternatives"

1. **"Just Like Heaven"** by the Cure
2. **"True Faith"** by New Order
3. **"West End Girls"** by Pet Shop Boys
4. **"A Little Respect"** by Erasure
5. **"You Spin Me Round (Like a Record)"** by Dead or Alive
6. **"Love Plus One"** by Haircut 100
7. **"I Melt with You"** by Modern English
8. **"Relax"** by Frankie Goes to Hollywood
9. **"Sex (I'm a . . .)"** by Berlin
10. **"Situation"** by Yaz
11. **"Tainted Love"** by Soft Cell
12. **"Need You Tonight"** by INXS
13. **"People Are People"** by Depeche Mode
14. **"How Soon Is Now?"** by the Smiths
15. **"Lips Like Sugar"** by Echo and the Bunnymen

The ever-peaked Robert Smith of the Cure

"Let me hear your body talk"

1981 was the Year of the Hot and Sweaty: The former *Barbarella* Barbie doll *qua* war protester (and future Ted Turner shadow) had a runaway bestseller with *The Jane Fonda Workout Book*; the latter-day Freud, Dr. Ruth, had the nation talking about sex (even if we were only wondering whether she ever got any); and **Olivia Newton-John's "Physical"** soared to the top of the charts for an astounding nine weeks.

The end result of all this? For the rest of the decade, we got to witness Richard Simmons prance around in his short-shorts and shed tears, if not pounds, with the nation's obese.

Richard Simmons, surrounded by a different kind of balloon

You'd think that the Motion Picture Association of America had passed an ordinance in 1980 that said a movie had to have at least one Top Forty hit on its sound track to qualify for release. But let's be thankful. Who'd want to live in a world where "Who's Johnny" by El DeBarge had no reason to exist? Ah yes, *Short Circuit*—that cinematic tour de force. But even better was *Short Circuit 2,* the stunning sequel where '80s movie juggernauts Steve Guttenberg and Ally Sheedy bowed out of their starring roles leaving just that Indian guy and the irrepressible No. Five. Listed in this section are the ten best lines from songs that appeared in movies. There were literally hundreds of choices, so no angry e-mails if we left off your favorite. (Sorry, Bette Midler fans.)

1. "Until we dance into the fire"

2. "The moon. Beautiful. The sun. Even more beautiful"

3. "Two by two their bodies become one"

4. "Take me to the action, take me to the track"

5. "Pictures come alive, you can dance right through your life"

6. "Kick off your Sunday shoes"

7. "Went to the beach, gave me a peach"

8. "Here we are hanging on to strings of greens and blues"

9. "'Cause every time he pulls me near, I just wanna cheer"

10. "And smiled in her special way"

Making Movies

In case you're wondering, here's our working definition of a **Brat Pack member** (brăt păk mĕm′bər) *n.* **1.** Twentysomething film star of the 1980s. **2.** Actor or actress appearing in either a John Hughes film or a movie named after a nautical phenomenon. **3.** Actor or actress whose limited acting ability led to a virtual disappearance from feature films (or led to radical cosmetic surgery) long before the fall of the Berlin Wall.

1. "Rain keeps falling, rain keeps falling down"
2. "Caroline laughs and it's raining all day"
3. "I touch you once, I touch you twice"
4. "If you want me, you can find me"
5. "You broke the boy in me, but you won't break the man"

SAINT ELMO'S BAR

Attack of the Brat Pack

1. **"Don't You (Forget About Me)"** by Simple Minds
   from *The Breakfast Club*

2. **"Pretty in Pink"** by Psychedelic Furs from *Pretty in Pink*

3. **"If You Leave"** by Orchestral Manoeuvres in the Dark
   (OMD) from *Pretty in Pink*

4. **"Left of Center"** by Suzanne Vega from *Pretty in Pink*

5. **"St. Elmo's Fire (Man in Motion)"** by John Parr
   from *St. Elmo's Fire*

"Babe you know you're growing up so fast"

If you turned on your radio in the summer of 1984, chances are it wouldn't be long before you heard **"Sister Christian"** by **Night Ranger.** If you turned on your TV around the same time, chances are you would have seen Mary Lou Retton or Carl Lewis racking up gold medals in the Summer Olympics. These two were on TV *all* the time, even after the damned Olympics were over. In fact, our researchers are still looking for a product that *wasn't* endorsed by the short, squat, troll-like Retton.

What is there to say about Madonna that hasn't already been said? Sure, we could make cheap jokes about nudie pictures, *Shanghai Surprise,* or breast-feeding, but we'll let you come up with your own. More than any other performer of the decade, Madonna elicited strong reactions from almost everyone—especially post-pubescent boys. But there's no denying that the blond-haired goddess was the most significant female entertainer of the decade. All this from a girl who used to sing backup for disco king Patrick Hernandez, who gave us "Born to Be Alive," perhaps the single worst recording in all of human history.

deities
of the
'80s

Madonna

1. "Honey, don't you fool around"

2. "I just think of you and I start to glow"

3. "Only boys that save their pennies
   make my rainy day"

4. "Been saving it all for you 'cause
   only love can last"

5. "I know I'm keeping my baby"

6. "Live out your fantasy here with me"

7. "I hold the lock and you hold the key"

8. "A man can tell a thousand lies"

9. "Where a girl loves a boy, and a boy
   loves a girl"

10. "I have no choice, I hear your voice"

1. "Borderline"
2. "Lucky Star"
3. "Material Girl"
4. "Like a Virgin"
5. "Papa Don't Preach"
6. "Into the Groove"
7. "Open Your Heart"
8. "Live to Tell"
9. "La Isla Bonita"
10. "Like a Prayer"

"In the midnight hour, she cried 'more, more, more'"

Annoying to the hilt, the platinum-blond rocker **Billy Idol** had a hit with **"Rebel Yell"** in 1984. And here's a trivia question for you: What band did this singer start his career with? The answer is Generation X. Congratulations, give yourself a wedge or a piece of pie or whatever it is you called that colored plastic Trivial Pursuit triangle.

Perhaps Idol, when he wasn't trashing hotel rooms or getting into motorcycle accidents, was one of those losers who memorized all the answers to impress their friends.

"Bollocks! Science and Nature again!"

Apparently, successful artists of the '80s felt it was their obligation to give something back to their communities. There was Live Aid, Farm Aid, and ten Jerry Lewis telethons. And that's not to mention the rash of recordings for various causes by Various Artists—the most memorable of which was USA for Africa, America's rip-off of the United Kingdom's Band Aid. Written by Michael Jackson and Lionel Richie, "We Are the World" brought together musical legends like Ray Charles and Bob Dylan with pop superstars like Cyndi Lauper and Tina Turner. Even Dan Aykroyd showed up for the occasion. No one's quite sure why.

1. "It's true we'll make a better day just you and me"

2. "Well tonight thank God it's them instead of you"

3. "We're stabbing our brothers and sisters in the back"

4. "Keep smiling, keep shining"

5. "United we stand, divided we fall"

6. "Who cries for the children? I do"

Artists United Against Whatever

1. **"We Are the World"** by USA for Africa
2. **"Do They Know It's Christmas?"** by Band Aid
3. **"Sun City"** by Artists United Against Apartheid
4. **"That's What Friends Are For"** by Dionne and Friends
5. **"Hands Across America"** by Voices of America
6. **"We're Stars"** by Hear n' Aid

"You want a piece of my heart,
you better start from the start"

For guitarist Paul Dean, fourteen was a lucky number. After thirteen failed attempts with bad Canadian bands, Dean teamed up with singer Mike Reno and his array of headbands to form **Loverboy.** The band with the most self-aggrandizing name of the decade had a Top Forty hit with **"Working for the Weekend."**

In retrospect, it's impressive the band had as much success as they did given how stupid Mike Reno looked. But he was just one of many who sported the "workout look." Torn workout tops, leg warmers, and, of course, headbands were de rigueur for would-be hipsters between the years 1981 and 1984.

The '80s were a decade rife with love songs. We've listed lyrics from our Top Ten. Feel free to add your personal favorites to the list, but there'd better be at least one Air Supply song among them.

1. "You're a candle in the window on a cold, dark winter's night"

2. "I know just how to whisper"

3. "No one needs you more than I need you"

4. "I took for granted the friend I have in you"

5. "Oh—once in your life you find someone"

6. "You're the only one who really knew me at all"

7. "How could our love be so blind?"

8. "In my life there's been heartache and pain"

9. "Baby there's nothing in this world that could ever do"

10. "I don't wanna lose this feeling"

Sappiest Love Songs of the '80s

1. **"Can't Fight This Feeling"** by REO Speedwagon
2. **"Making Love Out of Nothing at All"** by Air Supply
3. **"You're the Inspiration"** by Chicago
4. **"The Search Is Over"** by Survivor
5. **"Heaven"** by Bryan Adams
6. **"Against All Odds (Take a Look at Me Now)"** by Phil Collins
7. **"Open Arms"** by Journey
8. **"I Want to Know What Love Is"** by Foreigner
9. **"When I See You Smile"** by Bad English
10. **"Eternal Flame"** by the Bangles

"I wish I was in Tijuana eating barbecued iguana"

If you thought lead singer Stan Ridgway's head popping out of a bowl of baked beans in the video for **"Mexican Radio"** was weird, keep reading. **Wall of Voodoo** formed in 1977 in Los Angeles to compose music for low-budget horror movies. To help pay the rent, the band sold sea monkeys and horse-racing tips. But their story gets even weirder. In 1982, a year before the band's one and only hit, bassist Bruce Morland quit to pursue a career as a circus strongman. When Ridgway left, the remaining members briefly considered joining Morland on a worldwide tour opening for Bitsy the Dancing Bear.

Well, we've given you the luxury of theme sections to give you clues to the songs and artists. Now try working without a net.

1. "Now in the street there is violence"

2. "Just for fun he says, 'Get a job'"

3. "Billy left his home with a dollar in his pocket and a head full of dreams"

4. "The time has come to say, 'Fair's fair'"

5. "There's a new wave coming, I warn you"

6. "Lenny Bruce is not afraid"

7. "Lookin' like a true survivor, feelin' like a little kid"

8. "I love her eyes and her wild, wild hair"

9. "Got a beat-up glove, a homemade bat, and a brand-new pair of shoes"

10. "It's poetry in motion"

11. "Here's a little song I wrote"

12. "There's nothing that a hundred men or more could ever do"

13. "I'm going to miss your love the minute you walk out that door"

14. "Don't take no rhythm, don't take no style"

15. "Josie's on a vacation far away"

All Mixed Up

An '80s Lyric Potpourri

Part I

1. **"Electric Avenue"** by Eddy Grant
2. **"The Way It Is"** by Bruce Hornsby and the Range
3. **"Young Turks"** by Rod Stewart
4. **"Beds Are Burning"** by Midnight Oil
5. **"Kids in America"** by Kim Wilde
6. **"It's the End of the World as We Know It (and I Feel Fine)"** by R.E.M.
7. **"I'm Still Standing"** by Elton John
8. **"Wild, Wild West"** by the Escape Club
9. **"Centerfield"** by John Fogerty
10. **"She Blinded Me with Science"** by Thomas Dolby
11. **"Don't Worry Be Happy"** by Bobby McFerrin
12. **"Africa"** by Toto
13. **"Please Don't Go"** by KC and the Sunshine Band
14. **"The Stroke"** by Billy Squier
15. **"Your Love"** by the Outfield

"Now I'm all grown up"

When **Janet Jackson** was a little girl, she wanted to be a jockey and win the Kentucky Derby. But her dream of becoming the next Willie Shoemaker was put on hold when she joined the Jackson family variety act at the tender age of seven. (Her dream died altogether many years later when she had to choose between silicone and saline, but that's another story.) In the late '70s, Janet landed several television roles, including a notable run as the precocious Penny on *Good Times*. In the '80s, she married James DeBarge, of the singing/dancing DeBarges, which was the '80s music equivalent of a Montague marrying a Capulet. Not surprisingly, the marriage was soon annulled, and though her first solo records didn't make much of a splash, 1986's **"Control"** was just one of six Top Twenty hits off the album of the same name.

So, what do two city slickers know about country music? Nuthin'. But even we remember the lines from these crossover country hits.

1. "Midnight, and I'm waiting on the twelve-oh-five"
2. "You're just a step on the boss man's ladder"
3. "The life I love is making music with my friends"
4. "Giddy-up a oom pa-pa oom pa-pa mow mow"
5. "I could have gone to Canada or I could have stayed in school"
6. "I love to hear the thunder; watch the lightning"
7. "Singles bars and good time lovers were never true"
8. "Just touch my cheek before you leave me, baby"
9. "Little things I should have said and done"
10. "I'll think of you each step of my way"

All Hat and No Cattle

1. **"Queen of Hearts"**
   by Juice Newton

2. **"9 to 5"**
   by Dolly Parton

3. **"On the Road Again"**
   by Willie Nelson

4. **"Elvira"**
   by the Oak Ridge Boys

5. **"Still in Saigon"**
   by Charlie Daniels Band

6. **"I Love a Rainy Night"**
   by Eddie Rabbitt

7. **"Lookin' for Love"**
   by Johnny Lee

8. **"Angel of the Morning"**
   by Juice Newton

9. **"Always on My Mind"**
   by Willie Nelson

10. **"I Will Always Love You"**
    by Dolly Parton

"Are you somewhere feeling lonely,
or is someone loving you?"

Lionel Richie, the quintessential balladeer of the '80s, started his career with the Commodores, jazzing out on such hard-funk classics as "Brick House" and "Machine Gun." Richie himself, though, was always a bit of a wimp. Don't forget, he wrote and sang the 1978 hit "Three Times a Lady," and that's about as wussy as it gets.

By the '80s, Richie's career exploded with a string of hits, including this one: **"Hello."** The maudlin video starred a beautiful blind girl who creates a bust of Richie that is almost as ugly as the man himself.

Bruce Springsteen

Was there a more ubiquitous sight in 1984 than Springsteen's denim-clad derrière? Not only was it featured front and center on the cover of the *Born in the U.S.A.* album, but everyone across America got to see him shake it in the "Dancing in the Dark" video (directed by Brian DePalma). At one point, Bruce pulls a starry-eyed adolescent Courteney Cox on stage to join him in one of the worst displays of dancing ever witnessed on television, *American Bandstand* aside. With its parade of singles, *Born in the U.S.A.* elevated Bruce to new heights of stardom. Impressively enough, his follow-up, *Tunnel of Love,* reached Number One without the aid of Springsteen's posterior.

Incidentally, children of the '80s should remember that Cox's first TV gig didn't come on *Friends* or even *Family Ties,* but on 1985's *Misfits of Science.*

1. "I went out for a ride and I never went back"

2. "At night I wake up with the sheets soaking wet"

3. "I'm sick of sitting 'round here trying to write this book"

4. "They're still here, he's all gone"

5. "This whole world is out there just trying to score"

6. "He could throw that speedball by you, make you look like a fool, boy"

7. "And you give me a look-a like I'm way out of bounds"

8. "So tell me what I see when I look in your eyes"

9. "In '65 tension was running high at my high school"

10. "We're wipin' our fingers on a Texaco road map"

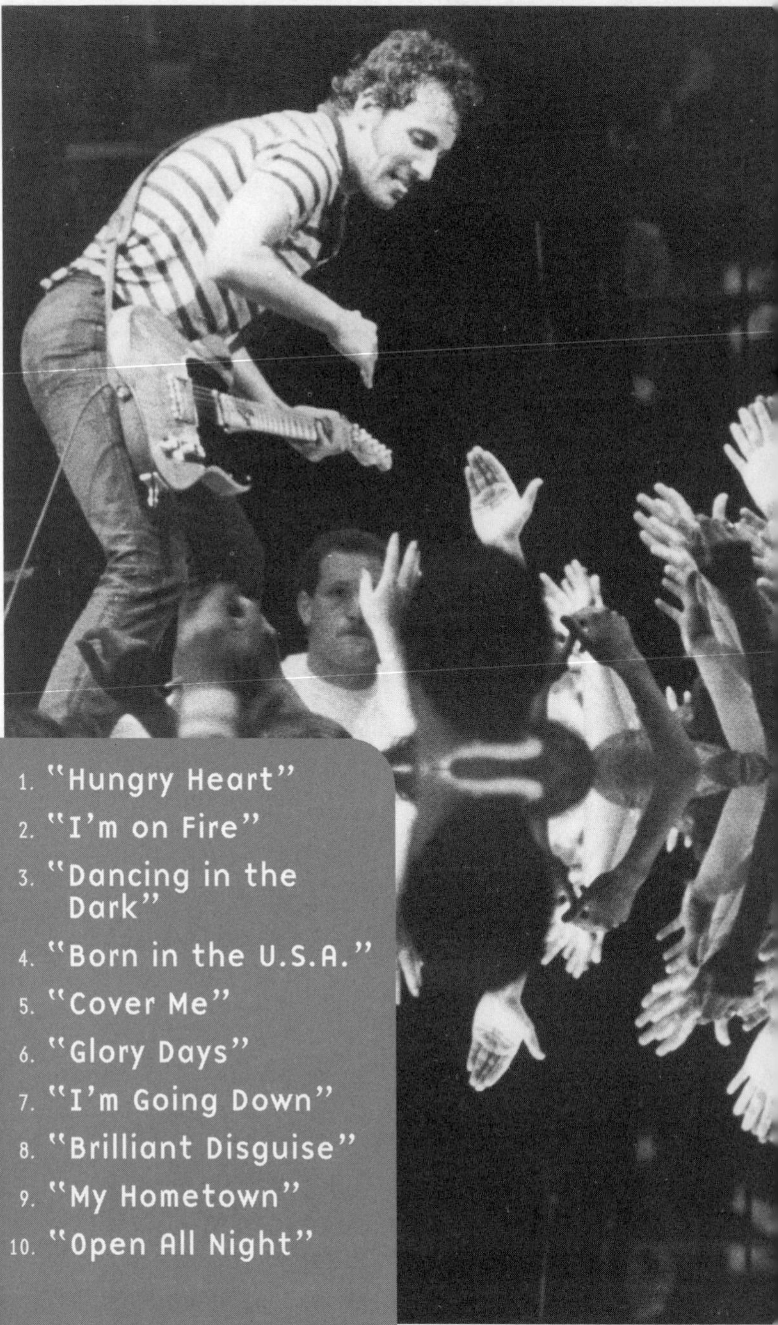

1. "Hungry Heart"
2. "I'm on Fire"
3. "Dancing in the Dark"
4. "Born in the U.S.A."
5. "Cover Me"
6. "Glory Days"
7. "I'm Going Down"
8. "Brilliant Disguise"
9. "My Hometown"
10. "Open All Night"

"We're living in a powder keg and giving off sparks"

Q. What do **Bonnie Tyler's "Total Eclipse of the Heart,"** Air Supply's "Making Love Out of Nothing at All," and a 300-pound ham have in common?

A. Writer/producer Jim Steinman.

Jim Steinman and Meat Loaf had a huge hit with *Bat Out of Hell* in 1977. Steinman's initial follow-up projects didn't live up to that success (his solo album, *Bad for Good*, was trashed by one reviewer in just three words: "Good for *nothing*"), but by October 1983, Steinman was back at the top of the charts. His ridiculously overwrought "Making Love Out of Nothing at All" by Air Supply almost made it to Number One. The reason it didn't: Another ridiculously overwrought Steinman hit, "Total Eclipse of the Heart," was holding steady at the top spot.

It's Saturday night and you're all decked out in your pastel blue sport coat, canary yellow shirt, and skinny piano-key tie. You see her across the room: torn pink warm-up suit top, Benetton skirt, and leg warmers. You finally work up enough courage to ask her to dance. Chances are, one of the songs listed below was playing when you busted your move.

1. "Looking from a window above"
2. "Let's dance in style, let's dance for a while"
3. "Knockin' me out with those American thighs"
4. "So put another dime in the jukebox, baby"
5. "Everybody had matching towels"
6. "Shotgun, get it done, come on..."
7. "And all my instincts, they return"

High School Dance Hits

"She dashed by me in painted-on jeans"

Billy Ocean (aka Leslie Sebastian Charles, aka the Caribbean King, aka the Love Man) was a poor man's Barry White for the '80s. We chose a lyric from **"Caribbean Queen (No More Love on the Run)"** because it was a Number One hit in 1984. But really, Billy's most inspiring line of the decade was from the lyrically complex "Loverboy," which contained such bits of poetry as "I say yeah yeah yeah-yeaaaah."

In 1985, "Caribbean Queen" enjoyed a resurgence because it was featured in the two-hour season premiere of *Miami Vice*. Ocean, a former tailor, was a natural for the show. His clothes were almost as garish as the threads worn by Don Johnson and Philip Michael Thomas.

The best TV crime-fighting duo of the decade wasn't Stephanie Zimbalist and Pierce Brosnan as Laura Holt and Remington Steele, but David Hasselhoff and William Daniels as Michael Knight and KITT. Basically, *Knight Rider* was *The Six Million Dollar Man* meets *Smokey and the Bandit*. With the royalties from this book, we hope to buy an '82 black Pontiac Trans Am and hire William Daniels to hide in our specially made compartment and give us directions ("Turn left here, guys"). Anyway, here are ten lines from songs featured in various TV shows and commercials.

1. "If you stay I'd subtract twenty years from my life"

2. "Been in trouble with the law since the day they was born"

3. "Taking a break from all your worries sure would help a lot"

4. "You be cool for twenty hours and I'll pay you twenty grand"

5. "Believe it or not, it's just me"

6. "I'm coming down, coming down, like a monkey"

7. "Got tired of packing and unpacking"

8. "Some walk by night, some fly by day"

9. "I've been waiting for this moment all my life"

10. "I got a crazy teacher, he wears dark glasses"

Songs
from the Tube

1. **"At This Moment"** by Billy Vera and the Beaters
   (as featured in *Family Ties*)

2. **"Theme from *The Dukes of Hazzard* (Good Ol' Boys)"** by Waylon Jennings

3. **"Where Everybody Knows Your Name"** by Gary Portnoy (*Cheers*)

4. **"Smuggler's Blues"** by Glenn Frey
   (as featured in *Miami Vice*)

5. **"Theme from *Greatest American Hero* (Believe It or Not)"** by Joey Scarbury

6. **"Tonight, Tonight, Tonight"** by Genesis
   (as featured in a Michelob commercial)

7. **"WKRP in Cincinnati (Main Theme)"** by Steve Carlisle

8. **"Moonlighting"** by Al Jarreau

9. **"In the Air Tonight"** by Phil Collins
   (as featured in *Miami Vice*)

10. **"The Future's So Bright, I Gotta Wear Shades"** by Timbuk 3 (as featured in *Head of the Class*)

"Me love you long time"

This line from **"Me So Horny"** by **2 Live Crew** (sampled from Stanley Kubrick's *Full Metal Jacket*) holds the distinction of appearing on a recording (*As Nasty as They Wanna Be*) that was declared legally obscene in 1989 by the great state of Florida. 2 Live Crew had been making incredibly offensive rap records for five years without anyone noticing. But all that changed when "moral crusader" Jack Thompson led the charge to have their album banned. The end result: An album destined for the clearance bin ended up selling over three million copies.

Whenever we hear "Jam on It" by Newcleus, it instantly conjures up images of break dancing: body poppin', top-rockin', the snake, the moonwalk, the head spin. And of course, break-dancing garb: Adidas, fat laces, and parachute pants. Break dancing was so hot in the early '80s that you could even take lessons—that is, if you wanted to.

1. "More punks I smoke, yo, my rep gets bigger"

2. "You're standin' on the wall like you was Poindexter"

3. "Posse in effect, hangin' out is always hype"

4. "Pound for pound, costs more than gold"

5. "I like the way they dribble up and down the court"

6. "To rock a rhyme that's right on time"

7. "You go to school to learn, not for a fashion show"

8. "She needs a guy like me with a high IQ"

9. "Elvis was a hero to most, but he never meant shit to me"

10. "They like to wear leather jackets, chains, and spikes"

11. "We rocked his butt with a twelve-inch cut"

12. "Better make it fast or else I'm gonna get pissed"

1. **"Straight Outta Compton"** by N.W.A

2. **"Bust a Move"** by Young MC

3. **"Wild Thing"** by Tone-Lōc

4. **"White Lines"** by Grandmaster Flash and
   the Furious Five

5. **"Basketball"** by Kurtis Blow

6. **"It's Tricky"** by Run-D.M.C.

7. **"Parents Just Don't Understand"**
   by D.J. Jazzy Jeff and the Fresh Prince

8. **"Roxanne, Roxanne"** by U.T.F.O.

9. **"Fight the Power"** by Public Enemy

10. **"Freaks Come Out at Night"** by Whodini

11. **"Jam on It"** by Newcleus

12. **"Push It"** by Salt-n-Pepa

Tina Turner

It's impressive that '60s star Tina Turner was even *alive* in the '80s, let alone a huge recording star. As she chronicled in her 1986 bestselling book, *I, Tina,* she had to deal with years of abuse from her infamous husband, Ike, and we're not talking about just putting up with his bad Afro. Nonetheless, Tina's '80s comeback was one of the major musical stories of the decade. She went from using food stamps in 1976 to sweeping the Grammys in 1985. Also in 1985, Tina resumed her acting career (remember her as the Acid Queen in 1975's *Tommy*?), costarring with Mel Gibson in *Mad Max Beyond Thunderdome*. She played Aunty Entity. She also sang two songs on the film's sound track, including the movie's theme—lines from both are listed below.

1. "Out of the ruins, out from the wreckage"

2. "You don't look at their faces and you don't ask their name"

3. "Who needs a heart when a heart can be broken?"

4. "Should I be fractured by your lack of devotion?"

5. "Who's gonna make it tonight?"

6. "Some boys think they're God's gift to woman"

7. "All I want is a little reaction"

8. "I can feel it but I can't let go"

9. "I hang on every word you say"

10. "When we were together everything was so grand"

1. "We Don't Need Another Hero (Thunderdome)"
2. "Private Dancer"
3. "What's Love Got to Do with It"
4. "Better Be Good to Me"
5. "One of the Living"
6. "What You Get Is What You See"
7. "Typical Male"
8. "Two People"
9. "The Best"
10. "I Can't Stand the Rain"

'80s Mystery Guest: Who Am I?

"Well, some people ain't no damn good"

I was born in America's heartland with the rare neurological condition spina bifida. My early bands included Crepe Sole and Trash, and in 1976, I released my debut solo album after David Bowie's manager made me change my name. I have a tattoo of a bearded lady on my right arm. In 1982, I won a Grammy for Best Rock Vocal: Male, with a song that some people thought had S&M overtones. After that, I changed my name again, helped organize Farm Aid, had a bunch of other hits, and then changed my name one last time. But most people will know me from these Top Five hits: "Hurts So Good," "Jack and Diane," and "R.O.C.K. in the U.S.A." . . .

... and, of course, this Top Ten song, **"Crumbling Down."**
I am **John Mellencamp,** at least for now.

"All the boys think she's a spy"

What was the bestselling single of 1981? **"Bette Davis Eyes"** by **Kim Carnes.** What was the bestselling novel? Stephen King's *Cujo*. What was the top-grossing movie? *Raiders of the Lost Ark*. And what was the bestselling puzzle? Rubik's Cube. Designed by Hungarian engineer Erno Rubik, the Rubik's Cube became such a national obsession over the next few years that at one point there were three bestselling books about the puzzle. Why anyone would want to buy a book on how to solve the cube when you could just take it apart and put it back together is beyond us.

Billy Joel was one busy piano man in the '80s. Consider the following: In 1985, as we all know, Joel married supermodel Christie Brinkley. But that wasn't his only major achievement. Throughout the decade, Joel toured extensively all over the United States, and in 1987 he went

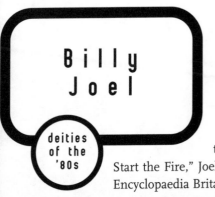

behind the Iron Curtain for a historic series of glasnost-inspired concerts. (Apparently, the line for concert tickets in Moscow was exceeded only by the line for government-issued toilet paper.) Oh yeah, and he also released nine albums, including *Storm Front*, which spawned the Number One hit "We Didn't Start the Fire," Joel's landmark collaboration with Encyclopaedia Britannica.

1. "I told you dirty jokes until you smiled"

2. "But here you are in the ninth, two men out and three men on"

3. "Out in Bethlehem they're killing time"

4. "But a nice girl wouldn't tell you what you should do"

5. "Are you gonna cruise the miracle mile?"

6. "I forgot how nice romance is"

7. "I thought I was the Duke of Earl when I made it with a red-haired girl"

8. "You know I can't afford to buy her pearls"

9. "Then it's the best feeling I've ever known"

10. "Starkweather Homicide, Children of Thalidomide"

"Now I see the road is bent"

How does one go from singing at the Met to the top of the pop charts? Ask **Debbie Gibson** (who was, by the way, Jim Scaduto's date at one of our high school proms). This chapeau-wearing teen soared to Number Four in 1987 with the nauseatingly sweet **"Only in My Dreams."** In her '90s incarnation as a "respected" Broadway actress (she has appeared in *Les Misérables* and *Beauty and the Beast*), Debbie Gibson has become "Deborah Gibson." If you penned the lyrics to "Only in My Dreams," wouldn't you want a new identity, too?

Before Hanson there were . . .
Four kid bands who had success in the '80s:

1. "I got a girl who cares who you like"
2. "Gotta catch that train at 7:30"
3. "How does it feel when you've got no food?"
4. "Everybody's always talkin' 'bout who's on top"

Young Turds

1. **"Cool It Now"** by New Edition
2. **"If You're Not Here"** by Menudo
3. **"Pass the Dutchie"** by Musical Youth
4. **"Hangin' Tough"** by New Kids on the Block

New Kids on the Block: Apparently this look passed for tough in Massachusetts circa 1989

"I got my first real six-string"

Bryan Adams was the most successful Canadian artist of the '80s. Of course, that's kind of like music's version of being the nicest guy in prison. Nonetheless, the former Bachman-Turner Overdrive and Juice Newton songwriter went on to have a number of hits, including "Run to You," "Cuts Like a Knife," and **"Summer of '69."** In 1986, he refused to allow his song "Only the Strong Survive" to be used in the smash hit film *Top Gun* because he felt that the film glorified war. In the '90s, however, he didn't seem to mind that his ballad "(Everything I Do) I Do It for You" appeared in the Kevin Costner movie *Robin Hood*, which glorified stealing.

Why is it that TV and movie personalities feel it's their God-given right to record albums? The '60s had the spaced-out rock poetry of William Shatner, the '70s had the heavily overdubbed ditties of Leif Garrett, and the '80s had the following lines from various soap opera, television, and movie stars:

1. "Kissing you was not what I had planned"

2. "You know he'll only use you up"

3. "Just a fool to believe I have anything she needs"

4. "See her shake on the movie screen, Jimmy Dean!"

5. "We don't have to be one or the other"

6. "And they've never heard of love"

Don't Quit Your Day Job

1. **"All I Need"** by Jack Wagner *(General Hospital)*
2. **"Don't Talk to Strangers"** by Rick Springfield *(General Hospital)*
3. **"She's Like the Wind"** by Patrick Swayze *(Dirty Dancing)*
4. **"Rock On"** by Michael Damian *(The Young and the Restless)*
5. **"Friends and Lovers"** by Gloria Loring *(Days of Our Lives)* & Carl Anderson
6. **"They Don't Know"** by Tracey Ullman *(The Tracey Ullman Show)*

"1773, he writes his first piano concerto"

Falco once stated, **" 'Rock Me Amadeus'** was the worst thing that could've happened to me." We guess the former classical music prodigy preferred being the king of Austrian techno pop to being the guy who had a Number One hit about a slightly more famous classical music prodigy. Falco's other claim to fame came three years earlier when After the Fire had a Number Five hit with their English-language cover of his cult dance hit "Der Kommissar." Sadly, in 1998, Falco died a horribly premature death when his sports utility vehicle was obliterated by a fifty-seat bus.

All right, so there are no words, but how else could we get "Axel F" in here? We thought about writing out "Dun dun dun-de-dun dun dun . . ." but decided instead to let you match the '80s instrumental hits with the artists who performed them.

a. Mike Post

1. "Axel F"

b. Bill Conti

2. "Theme from *Miami Vice*"

c. Prince

3. "Rockit"

d. Jan Hammer

4. "Theme from *Hill Street Blues*"

e. Vangelis

5. "Batdance"

f. Harold Faltermeyer

6. "Chariots of Fire"

g. Herbie Hancock

7. "Theme from *Dynasty*"

At a
Loss for Words

Instrumental Hits of the '80s

1. "Axel F" ▶▶ f. Harold Faltermeyer

2. "Theme from *Miami Vice*" ▶▶ d. Jan Hammer

3. "Rockit" ▶▶ g. Herbie Hancock

4. "Theme from *Hill Street Blues*" ▶▶ a. Mike Post

5. "Batdance" ▶▶ c. Prince

6. "Chariots of Fire" ▶▶ e. Vangelis

7. "Theme from *Dynasty*" ▶▶ b. Bill Conti

"Just like the old man in that book by Nabokov"

"Don't Stand So Close to Me" was a hit for **the Police** in 1981. When the band recorded "Don't Stand So Close to Me '86" for no apparent reason, Sting changed this line to "Just like the old man in that *famous* book by Nabokov." Thus began Sting's descent into pretentiousness that continued when he named his second solo album... *Nothing Like the Sun*, after a Shakespeare sonnet, and culminated in 1996 when he wrote and sang "La Belle Dame Sans Regrets" entirely in French. There's no truth to the rumor that Sting is currently recording an album in Urdu inspired by James Joyce's *Ulysses*.

Je suis un artiste.

"*Hasta la vista, baby*"

Most guys think this line was first uttered by Arnold Schwarz-enegger in 1991's *Terminator 2*, but girls who were around in 1987 know better. **"Looking for a New Love"** was a Number Two single for that year's Grammy award–winning Best New Artist, **Jody Watley.** Watley's previous credits included being a dancer on *Soul Train* (she was a Don Cornelius favorite), a gig with Shalamar, and singing on Band Aid's "Do They Know It's Christmas?"

To her fans, Watley brought high fashion to dance pop, but to others, she was just an ersatz Janet Jackson without the famous siblings.

Michael Jackson

deities of the '80s

Michael—what happened? One minute you're the king of pop, the next minute you're a genderless, noseless, ageless albino freak. Let's take a look at Michael's career achievements versus his bizarre personal behavior:

Achievement	Incident of Bizarre Personal Behavior
1. His obsession with pop perfection on 1982's *Thriller*, one of the bestselling albums of all time.	1. His obsession with John Merrick—the "Elephant Man"—and his bones.
2. His pioneering accomplishments in music video, including being the first black artist regularly featured on MTV.	2. His pioneering ideas about human aging, including reports of his sleeping in a hyperbaric chamber.
3. He helped create social awareness for African famine relief by cowriting "We Are the World."	3. He helped create the Neverland Zoo Foundation for the Preservation and Breeding of Endangered and Other Species so he could watch his pet panther romp around in his backyard.
4. His career caught on fire in 1983 as *Thriller* became the Number One album in every Western country.	4. His hair caught on fire during the filming of a Pepsi commercial.
5. Scores of hit singles with the Jackson 5 and as a solo performer.	5. Scores of evening visits from his "special friends" at Neverland Ranch.

*Before
the
'80s*

*After
the
'80s*

1. "I'll be the freak you can taunt"

2. "So take my strong advice, just
   remember to always think twice"

3. "You're playin' with your life,
   this ain't no truth or dare"

4. "Let me take you to the max"

5. "Someone's always tryin'
   to keep my baby cryin'"

6. "I like lovin' this way"

7. "Now is the time for you and I
   to cuddle close together"

8. "Your butt is mine"

9. "I like the groove of your walk"

10. "Who am I to be blind?"

1. "Dirty Diana"
2. "Billie Jean"
3. "Beat It"
4. "P.Y.T. (Pretty Young Thing)"
5. "Wanna Be Startin' Somethin'"
6. "Human Nature"
7. "Thriller"
8. "Bad"
9. "The Way You Make Me Feel"
10. "Man in the Mirror"

"He moved a million hearts in mono"

Everyone knows this song, but if you recognize this line you really are an '80s junkie. Singer Kevin Rowland of **Dexys Midnight Runners** was so difficult to understand that the record company felt compelled to put a disclaimer on the lyric sheet—not that anyone bought the album in the U.S. anyway. But the single **"Come On Eileen,"** fueled by its goofy video, was a Number One hit. If you look for Dexy in the video, you won't find him. The band's name is actually a reference to Dexedrine. Judging from their antics on camera, it's safe to assume that the drug was the band's amphetamine of choice.

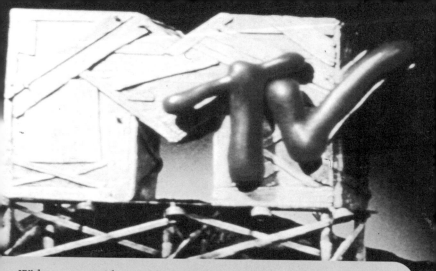

With so many videos to choose from, we're sure to offend everyone who reads this, but after careful consideration and forty-eight straight hours of viewing *Friday Night Videos, HBO's Video Jukebox,* and old MTV clips on a beat-up Betamax, here are lines from our Top Ten all-time desert island '80s music videos.

1. "When your dreamboat turns out to be a footnote"

2. "I've given up on this love getting stronger"

3. "Subtle innuendos follow"

4. "The sheik, he drove his Cadillac"

5. "I stumble into town, just like a sacred cow"

6. "You can act real rude or totally removed,
   and I can act like an imbecile"

7. "Step on a crack, break your momma's back"

8. "I think I'll dye my hair blue"

9. "I try so hard not to get upset"

10. "So I'll sing you a new song"

Music Videos

1. **"Everyday I Write the Book"** by Elvis Costello: *A dead ringer for Prince Charles literally jumps through a hoop of fire to win the affection of a Diana Spencer doppelgänger.*

2. **"Don't Come Around Here No More"** by Tom Petty and the Heartbreakers: *In this surreal video take on Lewis Carroll's drugged-out children's book, Tom Petty, as the Mad Hatter, takes a bite out of Alice in Wonderland.*

3. **"Goody Two Shoes"** by Adam Ant: *MTV's first guest VJ, Adam Ant, in his typically outlandish getup, denudes a prudish bookworm, revealing the surprisingly sexy vixen underneath.*

4. **"Rock the Casbah"** by the Clash: *Memorable images galore: A Hasidic Jew picks up a hitchhiking Arab in his big white Cadillac; the band plays in front of an oil rig; and an armadillo randomly scurries across the screen.*

5. **"China Girl"** by David Bowie: *A day at the beach for David Bowie and a hot Asian woman. This saucy video made waves at MTV because Bowie and his costar practically had sex on screen. MTV eventually aired a slightly less saucy version.*

6. **"Safety Dance"** by Men Without Hats: *Lead singer Ivan Ivan dances around the maypole with a peasant woman and their midget friend.*

7. **"Whip It"** by Devo: *Red flowerpot hats, a cracking bullwhip, and a leering band of cowpokes make this video seem weird even for Devo.*

8. **"Words"** by Missing Persons: *This would be a totally boring performance video if it weren't for lead singer and former Playboy bunny Dale Bozzio wrapped in cellophane.*

9. **"Voices Carry"** by 'Til Tuesday: *In this story video about a doomed couple—featuring lead singer Aimee Mann—a female musician's loser boyfriend (who appears in a wife-beater T-shirt in the opening scene) is more concerned with her haircut than with her.*

10. **"Hold Me Now"** by the Thompson Twins: *This video is so bad it's good. Lame special effects, horrible haircuts, and out-of-time clapping all combine to make this a quintessential '80s video.*

1. "Left right left, we all fall down"

2. "Don't want to end up a cartoon in a cartoon graveyard"

3. "Dial 'L' for love"

4. "Cryin' on the corner, waitin' in the rain"

5. "Brother's got a date to keep, he can't hang around"

6. "Things you do don't seem so real"

7. "I could give you all the loving you need"

8. "And she stood just like Bill Wyman, now I am her biggest fan"

9. "Are you ready? Hey! Are you ready for this?"

10. "Moving sidewalks, I don't see under my feet"

11. "Your legs are strong, and they're so, so long"

12. "The book of love will open up and let us in"

13. "I've never seen you looking so lovely as you did tonight"

14. "Bangin' on the bongos like a chimpanzee"

15. "Out on the road today, I saw a Deadhead sticker on a Cadillac"

All Mixed Up

An '80s Lyric Potpourri

Part II

1. "Toy Soldiers" by Martika
2. "You Can Call Me Al" by Paul Simon
3. "Word Up" by Cameo
4. "Harden My Heart" by Quarterflash
5. "Our House" by Madness
6. "She Drives Me Crazy" by Fine Young Cannibals
7. "Shake You Down" by Gregory Abbott
8. "Behind the Wall of Sleep" by the Smithereens
9. "Another One Bites the Dust" by Queen
10. "I Can Dream About You" by Dan Hartman
11. "So Alive" by Love and Rockets
12. "Broken Wings" by Mr. Mister
13. "The Lady in Red" by Chris Deburgh
14. "Money for Nothing" by Dire Straits
15. "The Boys of Summer" by Don Henley

"Oh, Daddy, dear, you know you're still number one"

Fresh from the New York rock scene and dressed like a young bag lady, **Cyndi Lauper** was a monstrous success in the '80s. Who could forget the video for **"Girls Just Wanna Have Fun,"** with Captain Lou Albano—he of the potbelly and rubber-banded beard—playing her father? Lauper's relationship with Albano led to the Rock and Wrestling Connection. In 1985, Lauper participated in one of the seminal cultural events of the decade, Wrestlemania. Perhaps inspired by Lauper, the World Wrestling Federation put out their own album featuring the vocal stylings of Hillbilly Jim and "Rowdy" Roddy Piper.

Under the stewardship of Lauper, Wendi Richter captured the W.W.F. Women's Title by defeating the Fabulous Moolah.

There were numerous Top Ten duet hits throughout the '80s, and, no, Jennifer Warnes didn't sing on all of them. But let's take a look back at Warnes's career: She got her start singing a duet with Donovan on *The Smothers Brothers Comedy Hour*. By the '80s, she managed to have incredible success doing one thing and one thing only: singing movie theme duets. Everyone remembers the Number One hits she had with Joe Cocker and former Righteous Brother Bill Medley. But did you know that she also sang movie theme duets with Chris Thompson (the title track from *All the Right Moves*) and Gary Morris ("Simply Meant to Be" from *Blind Date*)? She *even* sang a duet with Leonard Cohen ("Joan of Arc"). We're beginning to think this woman doesn't go to the bathroom by herself. Here are some other duets that topped the charts.

1. "Who knows what tomorrow brings"

2. "But don't play games with my affection"

3. "You have no right to ask me how I feel"

4. "I was there when they crucified my Lord"

5. "She's the kind of girl you dream of"

6. "Side by side on my piano keyboard"

7. "My love, there's only you in my life"

8. "Sail away with me to another world"

9. "I know you really want to be your own girl"

10. "Love, like a road that never ends"

11. "I'm glad they came along"

12. "What I want most to do is to get close to you"

13. "And you can count on me until the day you die"

14. "I swear that I can see forever in your eyes"

15. "And I never felt this way before"

Top
Duets
of
the
'80s

...and
Jennifer Warnes

1. **"Up Where We Belong"** by Joe Cocker and Jennifer Warnes

2. **"Say Say Say"** by Paul McCartney and Michael Jackson

3. **"Separate Lives"** by Phil Collins and Marilyn Martin

4. **"When Love Comes to Town"** by U2 with B.B. King

5. **"Easy Lover"** by Philip Bailey with Phil Collins

6. **"Ebony and Ivory"** by Paul McCartney with Stevie Wonder

7. **"Endless Love"** by Diana Ross and Lionel Richie

8. **"Islands in the Stream"** by Kenny Rogers with Dolly Parton

9. **"Stop Draggin' My Heart Around"** by Stevie Nicks with Tom Petty and the Heartbreakers

10. **"The Next Time I Fall in Love"** by Peter Cetera with Amy Grant

11. **"To All the Girls I've Loved Before"** by Julio Iglesias and Willie Nelson

12. **"Tonight I Celebrate My Love"** by Peabo Bryson/Roberta Flack

13. **"You're a Friend of Mine"** by Clarence Clemons and Jackson Browne

14. **"Almost Paradise . . . Love Theme from *Footloose*"** by Mike Reno and Ann Wilson

15. **"(I've Had) The Time of My Life"** by Bill Medley and Jennifer Warnes

"Telling lies, well, that's no surprise"

"Our Lips Are Sealed" by **the Go-Go's.** Well, apparently not. Long before the Pamela Anderson/Tommy Lee sex tape scandal, there was the "Go-Go's, Gone Gone" video extravaganza in which a pie-eyed Belinda Carlisle boasts about her various sexual escapades. Funny how Rob Lowe, whose best movie of the '80s lasted fifteen minutes and costarred a prostitute, played Balloonda's love interest in the video for the 1984 Go-Go's single "Turn to You."

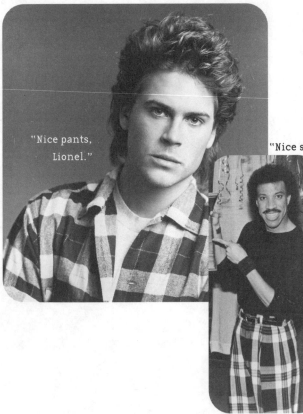

"Nice pants, Lionel."

"Nice shirt, Rob."

What a musical pedigree! When your mom is a famous gospel singer (Cissy Houston) and your cousin is Dionne Warwick, you're destined to have a successful music career, or at least unlimited free minutes on the *Psychic Friends Network*. And

Whitney Houston

deities of the '80s

Whitney's looks didn't hurt her either. Early on, the angel-faced diva had to choose between her music career and her modeling career. Obviously she made the right choice. Houston made pop music history in the '80s by releasing seven(!) singles in a row that reached Number One. Then, in 1992, she made a lot of men nauseous by marrying the former New Edition star and erstwhile king of kiddie funk, Bobby Brown, who miraculously had six Top Ten hits of his own in the '80s, despite having no discernible talent.

1. "Loving you makes life worth living"

2. "I say a prayer with every heartbeat"

3. "I've been in love and lost my senses"

4. "Sometimes life can make you crazy"

5. "Though I try to resist being last on your list"

6. "When all of my dreams are a heartbeat away"

7. "Ain't it shocking what love can do?"

8. "I believe the children are our future"

9. "I look in your eyes and I know that you still care for me"

10. "Now you're here like you've been before"

1. "Didn't We Almost Have It All"
2. "How Will I Know"
3. "I Wanna Dance with Somebody (Who Loves Me)"
4. "Love Will Save the Day"
5. "Saving All My Love for You"
6. "One Moment in Time"
7. "So Emotional"
8. "The Greatest Love of All"
9. "Where Do Broken Hearts Go"
10. "You Give Good Love"

"I'm not the kind of girl who gives up just like that"

With this tune, the downtown New York sound popped up from Pensacola to Peoria. Ah, the joys of mainstream success! People in Peoria still refer to Debbie Harry as Blondie, but—Illinoians, *please* pay attention here—**Blondie** is the name of the *band*. Debbie Harry should be referred to simply as Debbie Harry.

This lyric is from their reggae-rock cover, **"The Tide Is High,"** and the song's most notable achievement is that it landed Debbie Harry (not Blondie) on *The Muppet Show*.

Having trouble writing a hit song of your own? Record someone else's. Here are ten lyrics from cover songs that hit the charts. Can you guess who recorded the originals?

1. "If I leave here tomorrow"

2. "People know the part I'm playing"

3. "I know a guy who's tough but sweet"

4. "My best friend told me you're the best lick in town"

5. "You take a piece of me with you"

6. "There doesn't seem to be anyone around"

7. "Set me free, why don't you babe"

8. "It's tearing apart my blue, blue heart"

9. "Hey diddle diddle with your kitty in the middle"

10. "She's got it, yeah baby, she's got it"

Cover Me

1. **"Baby, I Love Your Way/Freebird Medley"** by Will To Power *(Peter Frampton/Lynyrd Skynyrd)*

2. **"Just a Gigolo/I Ain't Got Nobody"** by David Lee Roth *(Louis Prima)*

3. **"I Want Candy"** by Bow Wow Wow *(The Strangeloves)*

4. **"Once Bitten Twice Shy"** by Great White *(Mott the Hoople)*

5. **"Everytime You Go Away"** by Paul Young *(Daryl Hall and John Oates)*

6. **"I Think We're Alone Now"** by Tiffany *(Tommy James and the Shondells)*

7. **"You Keep Me Hangin' On"** by Kim Wilde *(The Supremes)*

8. **"Red Red Wine"** by UB40 *(Neil Diamond)*

9. **"Walk This Way"** by Run-D.M.C. *(Aerosmith)*

10. **"Venus"** by Bananarama *(Shocking Blue)*

"You really don't remember,
was it something that he said?"

The irrepressible
Ponch

Laura Branigan, who got her start singing backup with Leonard Cohen, was the female star of the decade until Madonna came along in 1983. Her biggest hit single, **"Gloria,"** off her eponymous 1982 album, was actually a remake of an Italian song (the eclectic limey Jonathan King also had a minor hit with it in 1979). Another Branigan hit, 1983's "How Am I Supposed to Live Without You," was written by the cheeze-metal-star-turned-balding-soft-rock-antichrist Michael Bolton. In that same year, Branigan joined the TV cop/future *telenovela* star Erik Estrada on an episode of *CHiPs.*

The irrepressible
Jonathan King

It's 1981 and double albums with four songs on them aren't selling anymore. So what do you do if you're an aging progressive rock star? You call up three of your aging progressive rock buddies and form a band that will take a decidedly different musical approach. The result: the corporate rock sound of Asia, which brought together Carl Palmer of ELP, Steve Howe and Geoffrey Downes of Yes, and John Wetton of King Crimson. Asia's success paved the way for other "supergroups" of the decade. After you've guessed the song and the band, see if you can name the significant members and which bands they came from.

1. "And now you find yourself in '82"

2. "It's never over and yesterday's just a memory"

3. "I'm gonna love you for the rest of your life"

4. "Reputation's changeable, situation's tolerable"

5. "Turn me on tonight"

6. "She wants to multiply, are you gonna do it?"

Supergroups

1. **"Heat of the Moment"** by Asia

2. **"High Enough"** by Damn Yankees: *Ted Nugent, Jack Blades (from Night Ranger), Tommy Shaw (from Styx)*

3. **"All I Need Is a Miracle"** by Mike + the Mechanics: *Paul Carrack (from Squeeze), Mike Rutherford (from Genesis)*

4. **"Handle with Care"** by the Traveling Wilburys: *George Harrison (from the Beatles), Bob Dylan, Jeff Lynne (from ELO), Tom Petty (from Tom Petty and the Heartbreakers), Roy Orbison*

5. **"Radioactive"** by the Firm: *Paul Rodgers (from Free and Bad Company), Jimmy Page (from Led Zeppelin), Chris Slade (from Manfred Mann's Earth Band)*

6. **"Some Like It Hot"** by Power Station: *Robert Palmer, Andy Taylor (from Duran Duran), John Taylor (from Duran Duran), Tony Thompson (from Chic)*

"Dressed up like a million-dollar trouper"

You got it! That's a line from **Taco's** abominable cover of the Irving Berlin classic **"Puttin' on the Ritz,"** a Top Five song in 1983. It was a surprise hit for the anachronistic Dutch performer who was born Taco Ockerse in Jakarta, Indonesia. One can only speculate how Taco (who sounded like a cross between Ethel Merman and Ringo Starr) developed such an obsession with American movies of the '20s and '30s. For the few fans who didn't get their fill of Taco from the "Puttin' on the Ritz" single, there were *two full albums* of Taco covering synthed-up old movie standards and singing heartfelt tributes to his favorite movie stars from sixty years hence. Eventually, Taco followed in the footsteps of his idols by embarking on a movie career. And while he didn't quite achieve the success of a Valentino or a Garbo, he did appear in the 1991 German movie *Karniggels* as "Man at party."

More tunes from the silver screen.

1. "Just a small town girl on a Saturday night"
2. "Let 'em say we're crazy, I don't care about that"
3. "No chocolate-covered candy hearts to give away"
4. "Say I'm old-fashioned, say I'm over the hill"
5. "She'll never know just how I feel"
6. "Watching every motion in this foolish lover's game"
7. "I am a man who will fight for your honor"
8. "Don't need no credit card to ride this train"
9. "Plastic tubes and pots and pans"
10. "What have I done today? Just sat and watched the jets fly over"

Part II

Making Movies

1. **"Maniac"** by Michael Sembello
   from *Flashdance*

2. **"Nothing's Gonna Stop Us Now"**
   by Starship from *Mannequin*

3. **"I Just Called to Say I Love You"**
   by Stevie Wonder from
   The Woman in Red

4. **"Old Time Rock & Roll"**
   by Bob Seger from *Risky Business*

5. **"On the Dark Side"** by
   John Cafferty and the Beaver
   Brown Band from *Eddie and the Cruisers*

6. **"Take My Breath Away"** by Berlin from *Top Gun*

7. **"Glory of Love"** by Peter Cetera from *The Karate Kid Part II*

8. **"The Power of Love"** by Huey Lewis and the News
   from *Back to the Future*

9. **"Weird Science"** by Oingo Boingo from *Weird Science*

10. **"I Go Crazy"** by Flesh for Lulu from *Some Kind of Wonderful*

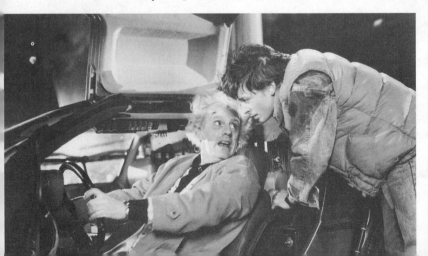

"On the boats and on the planes"

Neil Diamond: Who was VH1 before VH1 existed.

Picture this: It's a hot August night and the stage lights are burning. A gaggle of screaming fortysomething hausfraus are peeling off their undergarments and hurling them stageward at the hirsute-chested troubadour with the bad comb-over. You got it! You're front row center at a **Neil Diamond** show and he's belting out his biggest hit since "Sweet Caroline." **"America,"** featured in the awful remake of *The Jazz Singer*, got housewives out of the house and into the concert halls of America. Surprisingly, though, *Donahue*'s ratings didn't suffer.

Has any other decade seen such a preponderance of popular artists from two decades earlier cracking the top of the charts? In the list below you'll find lyrics from fifteen radio stars whom even video couldn't kill.

1. "All for a cuddle and a peck on the cheek"
2. "I remember skies reflected in your eyes"
3. "It's even worse than it appears, but it's all right"
4. "You might not be looking for the promised land"
5. "You better love me all the time now"
6. "Every time I look into your lovely eyes"
7. "City traffic movin' way too slow"
8. "I don't care if they start to avoid me"
9. "So we cheated and we lied and we tested"
10. "Well, lightning strikes, maybe once, maybe twice"
11. "Look inside your heart, I'll look inside mine"
12. "No dark sarcasm in the classroom"
13. "We'll get there fast and then we'll take it slow"
14. "You make a grown man cry"
15. "Feeling good from my head to my shoes"

Night of the Living Dead

'60s Artists with Hits in the '80s

1. "Come Dancing" by the Kinks

2. "Your Wildest Dreams" by the Moody Blues

3. "Touch of Grey" by the Grateful Dead

4. "Living in America" by James Brown

5. "You Better You Bet" by the Who

6. "You Got It" by Roy Orbison

7. "Freeway of Love" by Aretha Franklin

8. "Being with You" by Smokey Robinson

9. "Southern Cross" by Crosby, Stills and Nash

10. "Gypsy" by Fleetwood Mac

11. "Higher Love" by Steve Winwood

12. "Another Brick in the Wall (Part II)" by Pink Floyd

13. "Kokomo" by the Beach Boys

14. "Start Me Up" by the Rolling Stones

15. "New Attitude" by Patti LaBelle

Every member of the Beatles had at least one Top Forty hit in the '80s. Three of the four had Number Ones. Can you guess who didn't?

1. "It's like we both are falling in love again"

2. "You're my guiding light, day or night I'm always there"

3. "It's gonna take plenty of money to do it right, child"

4. "All dried up, I'm all dried up"

We Got the Beatles

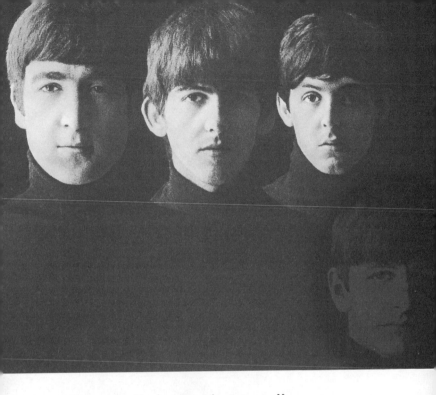

1. "(Just Like) Starting Over" by John Lennon
2. "No More Lonely Nights" by Paul McCartney
3. "Got My Mind Set On You" by George Harrison
4. "Wrack My Brain" by Ringo Starr

"I travel the world and the seven seas"

"Sweet Dreams (Are Made of This)" by **Eurythmics** was a Number One hit on September 3, 1983. It was Annie Lennox and Dave Stewart's first hit together as Eurythmics, but it wasn't the first time the former lovers hit the U.S. charts. Back in 1980, the two had a minor hit covering Dusty Springfield's "I Only Want to Be with You" with their band the Tourists. By the time Eurythmics blossomed, the two were no longer romantically involved. Stewart went on to marry one of the chicks from Bananarama. Lennox went on to marry a Hare Krishna who reportedly *really* liked her haircut.

More of a mascot than a pop star, Phil Collins (and Genesis) had scads of hits in the decade. You might also remember his guest appearance on *Miami Vice* playing a short, bald, English guy—not much of a stretch. His acting career supposedly got started as an extra in *A Hard Day's Night,* but we've watched the thing more than fifteen times and still haven't seen him. The peak of Collins's acting career came in 1988's appropriately named *Buster,* which would have disappeared even faster had it not

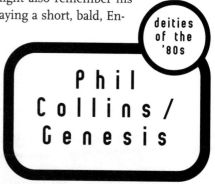

deities of the '80s

Phil Collins/ Genesis

been for Phil's two Number One hits off the sound track: "Groovy Kind of Love" and "Two Hearts." Phil's next Number One hit, the "socially aware" "Another Day in Paradise," was actually *the* last Number One song of the decade. In it, Phil didn't ask the yuppies of America to actually *do* anything about the country's problems, but he did ask them to "think twice." Thanks, Phil.

1. "Dance with me, you never dance with me"

2. "She's got something you just can't trust"

3. "I watch the world go 'round and 'round"

4. "Ooh, Superman, where are you now?"

5. "Turning me on, turning me off"

6. "They can turn off my feelings like they're turning off the light"

7. "'Cause you're not anywhere that I can find you"

8. "She's got blisters on the soles of her feet"

9. "Well, you can tell everyone I'm a darn disgrace"

10. "But I feel so good if I just say the word"

"Why do I find it hard to write the next line?"

Why did he find it so hard to write the next line? Probably for the same reason he found it so hard to write the next hit song, since **"True"** by **Spandau Ballet** was the band's only Top Twenty single in America. But this song definitely ranks as one of our guilty pleasures. Tony Hadley's crooning and the band's understated New Wave touch still sound surprisingly soulful for a bunch of English dandies.

"Tony, why aren't you wearing your ascot?"

You've already read about Nena, Taco, Dexys Midnight Runners, and numerous other "artists" who could be described as "one-hit wonders." Well, we've only scratched the surface. Here are our favorite one-hit wonders of the decade.

1. "You take me by the heart when you take me by the hand"

2. "I know a good thing must come to an end"

3. "I'm tired of listening to you talk in rhymes"

4. "I get my kicks above the waistline, sunshine"

5. "Hush hush, eye to eye"

6. "Feel like I could run away, run away"

7. "Your hair is brown, your eyes are hazel"

8. "I need you, I need you"

9. "I used to think maybe you love me, now baby I'm sure"

10. "Tell me, am I getting in too deep?"

One-Hit Wonders

"You'll be doing fine once the music starts, oh!"

DeBarge never quite fulfilled the expectation that they would someday rival the Jacksons as America's favorite family act. But siblings El, Marty, Randy, James, and Bunny did have a huge hit with **"Rhythm of the Night."** The video featured the fleet-footed, thinly mustachioed El, shimmying blithely in his convertible and on the street. This song's success prompted El to pursue a solo career, though he never quite fulfilled the expectation that he would someday rival Michael as America's favorite singing-dancing sideshow act.

FYI: In the spring of '85, when this song was at its peak, the Coca-Cola Company made one of the worst marketing decisions of all time (although chairman Robert Goizueta called it "the surest move ever")—they replaced Coke, which everyone loved, with New Coke, which everyone hated. In an effort to bolster New Coke sales, they recruited the supposedly computer-generated VJ Max Headroom to shill the swill.

It pays to have connections in the music business. Here are five performers who owe their success to nepotism.

1. "Back in the race, I'm movin' in"

2. "If I could I would"

3. "Who's playing tricks on me?"

4. "You can tell me any old thing"

5. "Ever since you've been leaving me I've been wanting to cry"

It's All Relative

1. **"Far from Over"**
   by Frank Stallone
   (Sylvester Stallone)

2. **"Break Down the Barriers"**
   by Simon Townshend
   (Pete Townshend)

3. **"Somebody's Watching Me"**
   by Rockwell
   (Berry Gordy)

4. **"Heart Don't Lie"**
   by La Toya Jackson →
   (Michael Jackson)

5. **"Too Late for Goodbyes"**
   by Julian Lennon
   (John Lennon)

"She's a very kinky girl"

Although **"Super Freak (Part 1)"** was a super fly tune, '90s jailbird **Rick James** deserved his time behind bars: Forget the abuse and drug charges, this guy was responsible for producing Eddie Murphy's insipid hit single, "Party All the Time."

James was back in the news in 1990 when the racehorse-ownin', baggy-pant-wearin' (and eventual bankruptcy-declarin') rapper M.C. Hammer allegedly stole "Super Freak" for his mega-hit "U Can't Touch This."

If you're going to be a singer, don't you think it's a tad pretentious to have your stage name mean "good voice" in Latin? For that matter, it's pretty pretentious to have your stage name mean *anything* in Latin. But apparently, nobody told that to Paul Hewson aka Bono Vox. Not that Dave Evans's stage name "the Edge" is any better. Nonetheless, the Irish quartet achieved critical and

deities of the '80s

U 2

commercial success in the early '80s. Then in 1986, Bono's ego officially joined the band, leading the way to a commercial explosion. By the decade's end, however, there was dissension in the ranks: Bono's ego actually replaced Bono himself, resulting in the band's fatuous efforts in the '90s.

At least Larry Mullen Jr. and Adam Clayton fought the urge to call themselves the Invisible Man and Ringo.

1. "I was on the inside when they pulled the four walls down"

2. "Broken bottles under children's feet"

3. "I want to be with you, be with you night and day"

4. "Early morning, April Four"

5. "I believe in the Kingdom Come"

6. "And when I go there, I go there with you"

7. "On a bed of nails she makes me wait"

8. "Over the counter with a shotgun"

9. "We need new dreams tonight"

10. "We got John Coltrane and *A Love Supreme*"

1. "I Will Follow"
2. "Sunday Bloody Sunday"
3. "New Year's Day"
4. "Pride (In the Name of Love)"
5. "I Still Haven't Found What I'm Looking For"

6. "Where the Streets Have No Name"
7. "With or Without You"
8. "Desire"
9. "In God's Country"
10. "Angel of Harlem"

"She's got hair down to her fanny"

How many gimmicks can one band have? Consider **ZZ Top's "Legs"** video: Between the beards, the hot girls, the souped-up cherry red 1933 Ford coupe, and the double-zee keychain, it's no wonder these guys exploded in the age of music video. In addition to the blues-rock fans and bikers who always showed up at their concerts, the '80s saw a new generation of MTV-watching ZZ Top fans who probably thought Muddy Waters was just another one of Uncle Bud's fishing holes.

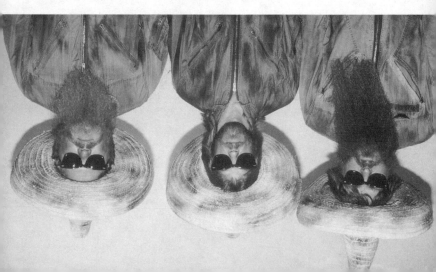

Six lyrics from artists who *owe* their careers (however brief they may have been) to music video:

1. "I just wanna tell you how I'm feeling"
2. "Don't switch the blade on the guy in shades, oh no"
3. "Or am I caught in a hit and run?"
4. "Aurora borealis comes in view"
5. "It's no better to be safe than sorry"
6. "'Cause as time goes by you've got to understand it's you"

Image *Is* Everything

1. Rick Astley's **"Never Gonna Give You Up"**: *If not for MTV...it's doubtful that this well-groomed, baby-faced crooner would have ever gotten an open-mike night gig, let alone a record contract.*

2. Corey Hart's **"Sunglasses at Night"**: *If not for MTV...it's unlikely that Hart, with his Tom Cruise rip-off Ray-Bans and his faux Elvis hair, would have wound up as a pinup on the bedroom wall of every teenage girl in America.*

3. Paula Abdul's **"Straight Up"**: *If not for MTV...she would still be kicking and jumping underneath the basket every time Shaquille O'Neal jammed one home.*

4. A Flock of Seagulls's **"I Ran"**: *If not for MTV...and a former hairdresser's own wacky hairdo (lead singer Mike Score who—surprise, surprise—had no musical background), A Flock of Seagulls would have spent the '80s playing in disco bars in Liverpool instead of living rooms across America.*

5. a-ha's **"Take on Me"**: *If not for MTV...and this band's amazing cartoon/live action video (and Number One hit in 1985), the Scandinavian answer to Duran Duran (and a bad one at that) would have missed their opportunity to be washed up by 1987.*

6. Milli Vanilli's **"Baby Don't Forget My Number"**: *If not for MTV...it's impossible that an out-of-work gymnast and a former break dancer—with hair extensions and socks stuffed in their bicycle shorts—could have lip-synched their way to a Grammy for Best New Artist of 1989.*

"We had broken up for good just an hour before"

"The Breakup Song (They Don't Write 'Em)" by **Greg Kihn.** With album titles like *Kihnspiracy*, *Kihntinued*, and *Citizen Kihn*, it's unclear whether his career wound down as a result of a lack of new material or a shortage of bad puns on his name.

Kihn's other hit, "Jeopardy," was brilliantly parodied by the vaudeville-style funnyman "Weird Al" Yankovic—one of the few people who seemed to know how comical the '80s really were while they were actually happening.

No, Alfred Michael Yankovic of Lynwood, California, is *not* related to the fabulous singing Yankovics of polka fame (or so he says). What we do know is that he *is* responsible for some of the funniest song titles of the decade (e.g., "I Want a New Duck" and "I Think I'm a Clone Now"). And, like so many of the Deities of the '80s, Weird Al used music videos brilliantly. His parodies of both Michael Jackson and Madonna were even more memorable than the original videos themselves. Weird Al's video success (not to mention his cameos in *Tape Heads* and *Naked Gun*) made him a natural to star in his own feature film, *UHF*, which did nothing at the box office, but did happen to star the pre-famous Michael Richards (Kramer from *Seinfield*) and Fran Drescher (*The Nanny*).

"Weird Al" Yankovic

1. "You play your bongos all the time"

2. "I took Potpourri for one hundred"

3. "I'm just an intern, I still make a mistake or two"

4. "There's Fortrel polyester, leather, wool and tweed"

5. "I've got more chins than Chinatown"

6. "Have some more yogurt, have some more Spam"

7. "All the soda jerkers know my name"

8. "I've often seen 'em whipped, but they just can't be beat"

9. "Can't play tennis and it's hard to bowl"

10. "Have-a some marinara, I know-a you like"

NAME THAT STAIN

SECRETS OF THE UNIVERSE

WORLD OF PHLEGM

THE YOUNG AND THE DYSLEXIC

1. "Ricky"
2. "I Lost on Jeopardy"
3. "Like a Surgeon"
4. "King of Suede"
5. "Fat"
6. "Eat It"
7. "I Love Rocky Road"
8. "Addicted to Spuds"
9. "Living with a Hernia"
10. "Lasagna"

It's January 1986 and you're surfing the dial on the car radio. At first you hear the usual suspects—"Say You, Say Me," by Lionel Richie, Whitney Houston's "How Will I Know"—but then you stumble onto something disturbing—a voice that's not exactly singing, not exactly rapping, more like mumbling. It's William "the Refrigerator" Perry of the Chicago Bears, and much to your disbelief "The Super Bowl Shuffle" by the Chicago Bears Shufflin' Crew is in the *Billboard* Top 100. In fact, this self-serving single stayed on the charts for almost two months. Mercifully, the Shufflin' Crew was never heard from again. Though the Bears may have demolished the Patriots in Super Bowl XX, in the long run they were no match for Duran Duran. Try your hand at these eight lines from novelty/humor songs:

1. "There's Sting looking for his last name in the dip"

2. "Your love is so edible to me"

3. "I got a pocket full of quarters"

4. "I called suicide prevention; they put me on hold"

5. "It's-a nice-a place"

6. "They call me 'Sweetness' 'cause I like to dance"

7. "Hey, Moe. Hey, Moe"

8. "They don't play baseball, they don't wear sweaters"

The Novelty Has Worn Off

Billy Crystal as Fernando

1. **"You Look Marvelous"** by Billy Crystal
2. **"I Eat Cannibals"** by Total Coelo
3. **"Pac-Man Fever"** by Buckner & Garcia
4. **"Rappin' Rodney"** by Rodney Dangerfield
5. **"Shaddap You Face"** by Joe Dolce
6. **"The Super Bowl Shuffle"** by the Chicago Bears Shufflin' Crew
7. **"The Curly Shuffle"** by Jump 'n the Saddle
8. **"Fish Heads"** by Barnes & Barnes

"The years go by, I'm lookin' through
a girlie magazine"

What do you get when you cross a blues musician, a record collector, an organist, and a DJ? The **J. Geils Band.** What did the J. Geils Band get when they replaced a piano with an '80s synthesizer sound? Two Number One hits, "Freeze Frame" and **"Centerfold."** But when lead singer Peter Wolf—the former high school dropout/painter/DJ husband of Faye Dunaway—left the band in 1983 to pursue a solo career ("Lights out, uh-huh") the J. Geils Band (even with a synthesizer) went the way of Faye Dunaway's movie career.

1. "Tonight's the night we'll make history"

2. "Do what they say, say what they mean"

3. "Now I'm towing my car, there's a hole in the roof"

4. "Shootin' at the walls of heartache, bang bang"

5. "One look at you and I can't disguise"

6. "So you better treat her right"

7. "You always live your life never thinking of the future"

8. "You could have a bumper car, bumping"

9. "Let me love you 'til the morning comes"

10. "Marvin, he was a friend of mine"

11. "Coast to coast, L.A. to Chicago"

12. "Take a look at my girlfriend"

13. "If I could reach the stars, I'd give them all to you"

14. "Just like Ronnie sang, 'Be my little baby'"

15. "And you want her, and she wants you"

All Mixed Up

An '80s Lyric Potpourri

Part III

1. "The Best of Times" by Styx
2. "One Thing Leads to Another" by the Fixx
3. "Don't Dream It's Over" by Crowded House
4. "The Warrior" by Scandal
5. "Hungry Eyes" by Eric Carmen
6. "She Works Hard for the Money"
   by Donna Summer
7. "Owner of a Lonely Heart" by Yes
8. "Sledgehammer" by Peter Gabriel
9. "Oh Sheila" by Ready for the World
10. "Nightshift" by Commodores
11. "Smooth Operator" by Sade
12. "Breakfast in America" by Supertramp
13. "If I Could Turn Back Time" by Cher
14. "Take Me Home Tonight" by Eddie Money
15. "No One Is to Blame" by Howard Jones

"They say you got a broken heart"

Well, this definitely isn't a line from **Bananarama's** 1981 song "Aie A Mwana." The lyric for that would be: *"Ti le pu le la pa tu"* since the song is sung entirely in Swahili. Rather, it's a line from **"I Heard a Rumour,"** the Number Four single off the trio's *Wow!* album. The band enjoyed tremendous success in England, and their cover of "Venus" reached Number One in the States. Not too shabby for a bunch of girls who couldn't play any instruments and never toured.

Incidentally, Bananarama took part of their name from the '70s kids' show *The Banana Splits,* though plans to cover the show's theme song ("One banana, two banana, three banana, four...") never came to fruition.

"I wanna tell her that I love her
but the point is prob'ly moot"

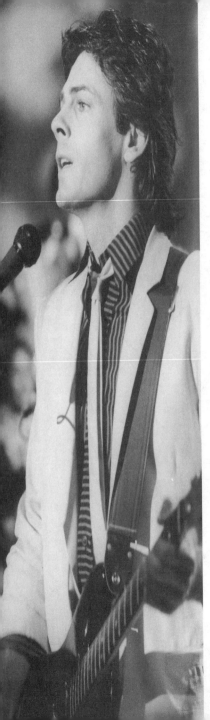

Pretty boy **Rick Springfield,** aka Dr. Noah Drake on TV's *General Hospital* (no, he wasn't Luke or Laura) had this Number One hit on August 1, 1981. Why else is that date significant? It's MTV's birthday. And music (or television for that matter) would never be the same. While MTV was airing its first video, "Video Killed the Radio Star" by the Buggles, a current TV star was Number One with **"Jessie's Girl."** The advent of music videos turned rock stars into TV stars and image became every bit as important, if not more so, than music. How else can you explain Milli Vanilli?

This time your task is to match the song with the celebrity who performed it. We'd give you lyrics, but we contacted all the celebrities below and even they couldn't remember them.

1. "Dreamin'"

2. "Heartbeat"

3. "Respect Yourself"

4. "Party All the Time"

5. "Let's Do Something Cheap and Superficial"

a. Eddie Murphy

b. Burt Reynolds

c. John Schneider

d. Don Johnson

e. Bruce Willis

Don't Quit Your Day Job

1. "Dreamin'" ▶▶ c. John Schneider

2. "Heartbeat" ▶▶ d. Don Johnson

3. "Respect Yourself" ▶▶ e. Bruce Willis

4. "Party All the Time" ▶▶ a. Eddie Murphy

5. "Let's Do Something Cheap and Superficial" ▶▶ b. Burt Reynolds

Bo (John Schneider), Luke, and Daisy Duke with the General Lee

"He just smiled and gave me a Vegemite sandwich"

The best new artist and biggest band of 1982, the Australian-based **Men at Work** sold millions of albums in a two-year span. At one point, both *Business as Usual* and *Cargo* were in the Top Ten on the U.S. charts. The group's two Number One singles were off their debut LP: **"Down Under"** and "Who Can It Be Now?" which, for those of you with a poor grasp of the obvious, is also the title of this book :-)

Gloria Fajardo grew up to be a Latina diva who ruled the '80s with hit after hit. She met her future husband, keyboardist Emilio Estefan Jr., in 1975 when she auditioned as a singer for his Miami wedding band. The band evolved into a major success as Miami Sound Machine. Ten years later, they were married, and their first all-English album, *Primitive Love,* went double platinum (by this time Emilio had moved from behind the keyboards to behind the scenes as Gloria's manager). By the decade's end, Gloria had broken sales records left and right, as well as one of the vertebrae in her back when her tour bus was blindsided by a tractor trailer. More hits followed, and Gloria went on to become the most successful Latina crossover performer of all time (sorry, Charo).

Gloria Estefan / Miami Sound Machine

deities of the '80s

1. "You make me feel so good"

2. "I know you can't control yourself any longer"

3. "And if you look in my eyes, we might fall in love again"

4. "Don't wanna be just your friend"

5. "Come on baby, say you love me"

6. "There's no place that you can hide"

7. "Don't you ever think that I don't love you"

8. "Baby when you're loving me, I feel like I could cry"

9. "Stand up and take some action"

10. "See who I am, and not who you want for me to be"

If the high school dance scene wasn't your style but you still wanted to get down, the '80s had plenty to offer. If your idea of a great Saturday night was standing behind a velvet rope outside of a dance club for four hours, then this section is for you. When you finally got inside, chances are one of the following songs was playing when a Donnie Wahlberg or Taylor Dayne look-alike asked you to dance.

1. "Just keep the groove and then he'll come back to you again"

2. "We do the dive every time we dance"

3. "Ladies love me, girls adore me"

4. "Is this really love or just a game?"

5. "Sex was something I just had"

6. "My heart does double beats for you"

7. "I, I like to feel the passion"

8. "Two hearts beating in time"

9. "Tell me now, take the initiative"

10. "Who do you want me to be to make you sleep with me?"

Shut Up and Dance

Dance Hits

"Those were the happiest days of my life"

"Back on the Chain Gang" was the biggest hit ever for Chrissie Hynde and **the Pretenders.** On April 3, 1982, when the song was peaking at Number Five, twenty-seven mayors nationwide, in an unprecedented attempt to woo voters' children, declared April 3 Pac-Man Day. Unfortunately for children in Phoenix, Arizona, local authorities refused to acknowledge the observance of Pac-Man Day simply because Pac-Man was yellow.

Before the popularity of Alanis Morissette, Fiona Apple, Tori Amos, Courtney Love, and all those other '90s Grrrls, there were . . . these less angry singing/songwriting females.

1. "They only hit until you cry"

2. "Speed so fast I felt like I was drunk"

3. "Philosophy is the talk on a cereal box"

4. "Lift my head from the pillow and then fall again"

5. "I went to the doctor, I went to the mountains"

Before Lilith Fair

1. **"Luka"** by Suzanne Vega
2. **"Fast Car"** by Tracy Chapman
3. **"What I Am"** by Edie Brickell and New Bohemians
4. **"Like the Weather"** by 10,000 Maniacs
   (featuring Natalie Merchant)
5. **"Closer to Fine"** by Indigo Girls

"Kiss me baby; let the fire get higher"

Steve Miller is one guy who's been around forever. He learned how to play guitar from Les Paul when he was in diapers. He played the Monterey Pop Festival in the '60s, broke out with a string of hit albums in the '70s, and had his third Number One song in the '80s. Shortly after **"Abracadabra"** by the **Steve Miller Band** hit the top of the charts in September 1982, college administrators nationwide enacted legislation requiring every college freshman to buy a copy of Steve Miller's *Greatest Hits*.

Part II

All right, so we couldn't resist listing ten
more of our favorites.

1. "For the price of a dime I can always turn to you"

2. "I never saw you look like this without a reason"

3. "I sailed away to China in a little rowboat to find you"

4. "I can lock all my doors"

5. "Too long ago, too long apart"

6. "Give a little bit of love to grow"

7. "Several years ago I said good-bye to my own sanity"

8. "And the children drank lemonade"

9. "Four . . . three . . . two . . . one . . . Earth below us"

10. "Blessed is the millionaire who shares your wedding day"

One-Hit Wonders

1. "867-5309/Jenny" by Tommy Tutone
2. "In a Big Country" by Big Country
3. "Break My Stride" by Matthew Wilder
4. "Cars" by Gary Numan
5. "The Captain of Her Heart" by Double
6. "Heart and Soul" by T'Pau
7. "I Don't Mind at All" by Bourgeois Tagg
8. "Life in a Northern Town" by the Dream Academy
9. "Major Tom (Coming Home)" by Peter Schilling
10. "Mary's Prayer" by Danny Wilson

"So bring your good times and your laughter, too"

Though it's hard to imagine Ronald Reagan getting down to **Kool and the Gang** ("Hey, Nancy, put on 'Jungle Boogie' again!"), **"Celebration"** became the nation's unofficial theme song with the release of the American hostages in Iran. If, heaven forbid, you want to hear this song today, just stop by a wedding reception—*any* wedding reception.

"Tommy used to work on the docks"

It had to be his good looks, right? How else could a big-haired working-class stiff from Sayreville, New Jersey, have *four* Number One records in the '80s? Jon Bon Jovi (Bruce Springsteen for Dummies) and his creatively named band **Bon Jovi** had a major hit with this anthemic and anathemic song **"Livin' on a Prayer"** from the *Slippery When Wet* LP—as if New Yorkers needed another excuse to hate the state of New Jersey.

Do you remember that chick in class with those white pleather boots, oversized belt, black leather jacket, and long, feathered hair? Well, this is what she was blasting out of the window of her beat-up Pinto while waiting in the parking lot before the Loudness/Mötley Crüe show.

1. "And the music makes her feel so hot"

2. "She's a killer at large"

3. "And the good book . . . it says we'll win"

4. "Oh yeah, I just wanna watch the girls go by"

5. "We're heading for Venus and still we stand tall"

6. "Daddy says she's too young, but she's old enough for me"

7. "Out there is a fortune waiting to be had"

8. "I've watched all the dropouts who make their own rules"

9. "I knew right from the start, you'd put an arrow through my heart"

10. "I never had a chance to love you"

Cheeze Metal Revisited

1. **"Little Suzi"** by Tesla
2. **"Midnite Maniac"** by Krokus
3. **"Soldiers Under Command"** by Stryper
4. **"Summertime Girls"** by Y&T
5. **"The Final Countdown"** by Europe
6. **"Seventeen"** by Winger
7. **"You've Got Another Thing Comin'"** by Judas Priest
8. **"Crazy Train"** by Ozzy Osbourne
9. **"Round and Round"** by Ratt
10. **"Wait"** by White Lion

"You make the sun shine brighter than Doris Day"

Were they or weren't they?

Wham!, the prefab '80s duo of ambiguous sexuality, consisted of onetime school chums George Michael and Andrew Ridgeley. The biggest of their many hits were Number Ones "Careless Whisper" (which featured their dark, moody, brooding side) and **"Wake Me Up Before You Go Go"** (which featured their bright, happy, playful side). Michael wrote and sang all the songs, and Ridgeley, well . . . nobody's quite sure what Ridgeley did other than drive expensive cars and show up in the gossip columns. This unbalance led to Ridgeley's dismissal in 1986, after which Michael went on to pursue a surprisingly successful career of his own (including a notable solo performance at Beverly Hills's Will Rogers Park in 1998). As for Ridgeley, we're still looking for a person on this earth who bought his 1990 solo effort *Son of Albert.*

Huey Lewis and the News

We're pretty sure Huey Lewis is the only one of our Deities of the '80s who got into Cornell. And he's certainly the only one who scored a perfect 800 on his Math SAT. (Of course, he did have an unfair advantage—what with his giant, square-shaped head and all.) But Huey's talents weren't limited to trigonometry and algebra: Huey and his backup band, the News, had seventeen Top Forty hits—most of them in the '80s. Lewis and his lawyers claimed that one of those hits, "I Want a New Drug," was plagiarized by Ray Parker Jr. in his Number One song "Ghostbusters." Listen to them back-to-back and you'll understand why Ray settled out of court.

1. "I was walking down a one-way street"

2. "I get a check on Friday, but it's already spent"

3. "Hot loving every night"

4. "Or make me feel three feet thick"

5. "DC, San Antone and the liberty town, Boston, and Baton Rouge"

6. "If this ain't love, you better let me go"

7. "We've had our doubts, we never took them seriously"

8. "You might think I'm crazy, but I don't even care"

9. "Step by step, one by one, higher and higher"

10. "It seems like everything I do I'm doing better"

1. "Do You Believe in Love"
2. "Workin' for a Livin'"
3. "Heart and Soul"
4. "I Want a New Drug"
5. "The Heart of Rock & Roll"
6. "If This Is It"
7. "Stuck with You"
8. "Hip to Be Square"
9. "Jacob's Ladder"
10. "Doing It All for My Baby"

"Who cares, they're always changing
corporation names"

Like many ex-hippies, Grace Slick spent the '80s making a ton of money. The commercial success that she enjoyed with **Starship** even surpassed anything she ever did with Jefferson Airplane. Still, it was kind of depressing to see the pioneering sex goddess who sang "White Rabbit" devolve into the aging sellout who barked the silly lyrics to **"We Built This City."**

If the thought of John Cougar Mellencamp singing "I Saw Mommy Kissing Santa Claus" makes you cringe, fear not. Listed below are seven lyrics from *original* Christmas songs of the '80s—one of which is quite possibly the "freshest" Christmas song ever recorded.

1. "Share the joy of laughter and good cheer"

2. "Give all the toys to the little rich boys"

3. "'Cause Christmas ain't the time for breaking each other's hearts"

4. "You mean you forgot cranberries, too?"

5. "You can say there's no such thing as Santa"

6. "Mom's cooking chicken and collard greens"

7. "We're here tonight and that's enough"

Yes, We Know It's Christmas

1. **"Christmas Is the Time to Say 'I Love You'"** by Billy Squier

2. **"Father Christmas"** by the Kinks

3. **"Merry Christmas (I Don't Wanna Fight)"** by the Ramones

4. **"Christmas Wrapping"** by the Waitresses

5. **"Grandma Got Run Over by a Reindeer"** by Elmo n' Patsy

6. **"Christmas in Hollis"** by Run-D.M.C.

7. **"Wonderful Christmas Time"** by Paul McCartney

"Your mom threw away your best porno mag"

The **Beastie Boys** were the first successful white rappers. Er, come to think of it, the Beastie Boys were the only successful white rappers. (Unless you count Vanilla Ice, whose success lasted about as long as Yahoo Serious's.) Their underground hit "Cookie Puss" landed the boys a gig opening for Madonna on her Virgin Tour. Not surprisingly, the band's atonal, profanity-laden set didn't go over so well with the 20,000 crucifix-wearing screaming teens in white lace. Despite their obnoxious demeanor and vexatious rapping, the Beasties broke out big time with *Licensed to Ill*— Columbia Records's fastest-selling debut album ever. And their signature song, **"(You Gotta) Fight for Your Right (to Party!),"** became an '80s high school keg party staple.

Yahoo Serious

"Oh, look what you done to this rock 'n' roll clown"

What do you call an English heavy metal band that has a drummer with one arm? Lefty. Nah, just kidding. You call them **Def Leppard,** of course. **"Photograph,"** off *Pyromania*—an album that sold over ten million copies—was the band's only Top Fifteen hit with a two-armed drummer. Two years after the release of *Pyromania*, drummer Rick Allen had his left arm amputated after he crashed his Corvette Stingray on an English road. But instead of kicking Rick's armless ass out of the band, Def Leppard thrived with the help of drum machines and computers. In 1987, they released their monster hit *Hysteria*, which gave the band six Top Twenty singles. Perhaps Krokus would have enjoyed more success had their drummer Jeff Klaven loaded up on extra-strength cold medicine before operating heavy machinery.

Hey, remember the guy and the girl we described on pages 23 and 185? Well, this is what they were listening to in the backseat of that girl's Pinto:

1. "As long as I'm the hero of this little girl"
2. "I should have known better than to let you go alone"
3. "Just like every cowboy sings a sad, sad song"
4. "What am I supposed to do with a childhood tragedy?"
5. "She's got eyes of the bluest skies"
6. "I can't tell you baby what went wrong"
7. "I'd like to see you in the morning light"
8. "Woke up to the sound of pouring rain"
9. "I got so much to learn about love in this world"
10. "After all this time, you still haunt my mind"

Heavy Metal Makeout Music

aka Power Ballads of the '80s

"Get my dinner from a garbage can"

Although their clothes and sound were straight out of the Eisenhower era, **the Stray Cats** were a surprise success with their neo-rockabilly hits in the Reagan era. While **"Stray Cat Strut"** was still in the Top Twenty in March 1983, Nancy "Just Say No" Reagan guest-starred on an episode of *Diff'rent Strokes* and offered Arnold the following cautionary tale: "Let me tell you a true story about a boy we'll call Charlie. He was only fourteen and he was burned out on marijuana.... One day, when his little sister wouldn't steal some money for him to go and buy some more drugs, he brutally beat her. ... Don't end up another Charlie."

"What'choo talkin' 'bout, Mrs. R?"

Duran Duran

deities of the '80s

With their fashionable good looks and impeccable makeup, Duran Duran were the envy of women all over the world—even Princess Diana was a fan. But in 1985, Duran Duran fans had a major scare. Lead singer and sailing enthusiast Simon Le Bon was involved in a serious boating accident when he dropped his favorite shade of lipstick into the Atlantic Ocean during the final race of the Admiral's Cup series. Actually, according to the August 12, 1985, *San Diego Union-Tribune*, "Le Bon was asleep below deck when the vessel's keel sheared off in 50-mph winds." Apparently, Le Bon was tuckered out from a hard day of sunbathing and entertaining the crew with a medley of his favorite sea chanteys.

1. "Straddle the line in discord and rhyme"

2. "It means so much to me—like a birthday or a pretty view"

3. "You're about as easy as a nuclear war"

4. "Lipstick cherry all over the lens as she's falling"

5. "I stayed the cold day with a lonely satellite"

6. "So why don't you use it?"

7. "They tried to break us, looks like they'll try again"

8. "And you wanted to dance so I asked you to dance"

9. "Don't monkey with my business"

10. "Your rhythm is the power to move me"

1. "Hungry Like the Wolf"
2. "Rio"
3. "Is There Something I Should Know"
4. "Girls on Film"
5. "New Moon on Monday"
6. "The Reflex"
7. "The Wild Boys"
8. "Save a Prayer"
9. "Notorious"
10. "I Don't Want Your Love"

"I'm about to lose control and I think I like it!"

Unlike the Thompson Twins, **the Pointer Sisters** were actually related. Bonnie, Anita, and June got their musical start (as did Mickey Thomas of Starship) singing with Elvin Bishop, who, despite being a blues-rock legend, also ran some sort of apprenticeship program for bad '80s pop stars. Ruth Pointer joined her sisters in 1972 for the recording of their debut album, and although they had some minor hits (they won a Grammy for Best Country [sic] Single), the sisters didn't have a Top Ten until Bonnie left in 1978. **"I'm So Excited,"** "Jump (for My Love)," and "Neutron Dance" were all Top Ten hits for the trio. When "Neutron Dance," featured in *Beverly Hills Cop*, was shooting up the *Billboard* charts on December 31, 1984, the vigilante gunman Bernhard Goetz was shooting up a band of screwdriver-wielding teenagers in a New York City subway.

"I'd drive a million miles"

Desmond Wang and Charles "Trip" Chung first met in the paddock at the Ascot Gold Cup in 1977. After sharing a Pimms and lemonade, the two decided to...Nah, just kidding. Actually, Jack Hues (pronounced "J'accuse") and Nick Feldman of **Wang Chung** met through a classified in the British music paper *Melody Maker*. In 1983, the band had a minor hit with the balladic "Dance Hall Days." But their biggest hit came two years later. **"Everybody Have Fun Tonight"** was so pervasive that even *Cheers* character Frasier quoted the song's profound philosophical couplet: "Everybody have fun tonight/ Everybody Wang Chung tonight."

'80s Mystery Guest: Who Am I?

"Why do you hurt me so bad?"

I was the most successful hard rock diva of the '80s. I was born with the last name of Andrzejewski in Brooklyn in 1953. Before I hit it big, I trained at Juilliard to be an opera singer, junked that to become a singing waitress, then refashioned myself as a cabaret singer. Just a few years later, I was so popular that my clothes and hair were copied by at least 40 percent of the high school girls in America. My tough gal signature "look" was even referenced in *Fast Times at Ridgemont High*. I won four Grammys for Best Rock Vocal: Female, and I had twelve Top Forty hits, including "Heartbreaker," "We Belong," and this one . . .

... **"Love Is a Battlefield."**
I am **Pat Benatar.**

Hall and Oates were *the* duo of the '80s. The lanky, blond Hall and the short, swarthy Oates teamed up for a string of R&B-flavored hits. Their best-of, *Rock 'n' Soul, Part 1,* went double platinum. Unfortunately for them, they never produced enough decent material to fill out a *Rock 'n' Soul, Part 2.* In fact, in the early '90s, while their former backup musicians G. E. Smith and T-Bone Wolk were busy grimacing every time *Saturday Night Live* cut to a commercial, the dynamic duo was nowhere to be found.

Radio execs attribute the duo's disappearance to their choosing the absolute worst album title of the decade for their 1988 effort: *Ooh Yeah!*

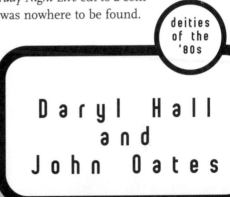

deities
of the
'80s

**D a r y l   H a l l
a n d
J o h n   O a t e s**

1. "But if you insist on knowing my bliss"

2. "What I want, you've got, but it might be hard to handle"

3. "You got the body, now you want my soul"

4. "Well, you can count on 'the kid'"

5. "The woman is wild, a she-cat tamed by the purr of a Jaguar"

6. "But if you push me too far, I just might"

7. "It seems I don't get time out anymore"

8. "But if I'm faced with being replaced, I want you even more"

9. "But I'm out of my head when you're not around"

10. "You play with words, you play with love"

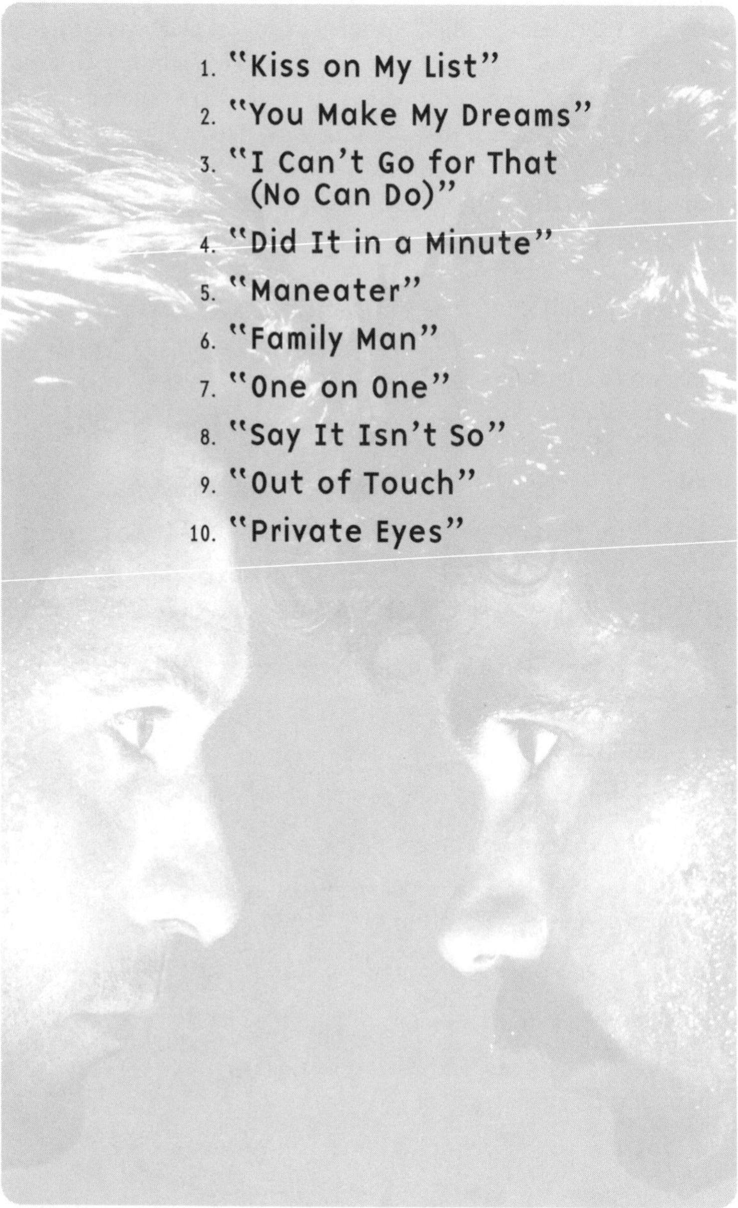

1. "Kiss on My List"
2. "You Make My Dreams"
3. "I Can't Go for That (No Can Do)"
4. "Did It in a Minute"
5. "Maneater"
6. "Family Man"
7. "One on One"
8. "Say It Isn't So"
9. "Out of Touch"
10. "Private Eyes"

"I said to my reflection, 'Let's get out of this place'"

"Tempted" by **Squeeze** didn't even crack the Top Forty, but it remains one of the enduring singles of 1981.

What do Pablo Cruise's "Cool Love," Lulu's "I Could Never Miss You," and Balance's "Breaking Away" all have in common? All of these cracked the Top Twenty-five when "Tempted" was peaking at Number Forty-nine.

Extra points for anyone who can name even one line from any of those other three.

In case you didn't believe us when we said the '80s were a decade dripping with sappy love songs, we've included ten more for your reading "pleasure." You know, for those long, cold, lonely nights when all you've got is a warm fire, a bottle of wine, REO Speedwagon's *The Hits,* and this book to keep you company. So dry your eyes and have a laugh at the lines below—and we mean that from the bottom of our hearts.

1. "Who would've thought that a boy like me could come to this"

2. "You were the first, you'll be the last"

3. "The love I'm sending ain't making it through to your heart"

4. "Everybody needs a little time away"

5. "I don't know how to stop feeling this way"

6. "Ooh, babe, lost in love is what I feel"

7. "When I said that I love you, I meant that I'd love you forever"

8. "We have the right you know"

9. "Is it so wrong to be human after all?"

10. "And it's my heart that's breakin' down this long-distance line tonight"

Sappiest Love Songs Revisited

1. (I Just) Died in Your Arms Tonight"
   by the Cutting Crew

2. "The Flame" by Cheap Trick

3. "What About Love" by Heart

4. "Hard to Say I'm Sorry" by Chicago

5. "Hold On to the Nights" by Richard Marx

6. "When I'm with You" by Sheriff

7. "Keep On Lovin' You" by REO Speedwagon

8. "The One That You Love" by Air Supply

9. "Something About You" by Level 42

10. "Missing You" by John Waite

1. "Kissing like a bandit stealing time"

2. "Come on, I'm talking to you"

3. "Your heart sweats, your body shakes"

4. "Who broke my heart? You did, you did"

5. "I'm gonna say it like a man and make you understand"

6. "Hold tight, wait 'til the party's over"

7. "Just a city boy, born and raised in South Detroit"

8. "I don't know why sometimes I get frightened"

9. "We only act like children when we argue, fuss, and fight"

10. "I don't need permission, make my own decisions"

11. "It keeps me standing still, it takes all my will"

12. "The thrill is still hot"

13. "I know that I'm right, 'cause I hear it in the night"

14. "Like a shot in the dark, when the going gets rough"

15. "No saints, no sinners, no devil as well"

All Mixed Up

An '80s Lyric Potpourri

Part IV

1. "Wishing Well" by Terence Trent D'Arby

2. "Shout" by Tears for Fears

3. "Addicted to Love" by Robert Palmer

4. "Poison Arrow" by ABC

5. "Amanda" by Boston

6. "Burning Down the House" by Talking Heads

7. "Don't Stop Believin'" by Journey

8. "I Got You" by Split Enz

9. "If You Don't Know Me by Now" by Simply Red

10. "My Prerogative" by Bobby Brown

11. "Suddenly Last Summer" by the Motels

12. "Solid" by Ashford and Simpson

13. "Talking in Your Sleep" by the Romantics

14. "Soldier of Love" by Donny Osmond

15. "Dear God" by XTC

How could a supposedly hip music book geared toward twentysomethings be complete without mentioning master tunesmith Burt Bacharach? It couldn't. Besides, any guy whose champion three-year-old filly of 1983 was named after one of his hit '80s songs gets props. Check out these five lines from Bacharach-composed hits.

1. "When you get caught between the moon and New York City"

2. "Let it shine wherever you go"

3. "How can I forget you, girl"

4. "So many times, said it was forever"

5. "I'll write your name in my book at least a thousand times"

Afternoon Deelites

Bacharach in the '80s

1. **"Arthur's Theme (Best That You Can Do)"** by Christopher Cross

2. **"Heartlight"** by Neil Diamond

3. **"There's Always Something There to Remind Me"** by Naked Eyes

4. **"On My Own"** by Patti LaBelle and Michael MacDonald

5. **"Love Always"** by El DeBarge

Mr. Bacharach also composed the Number One hit "That's What Friends Are For."

"Like my mother is like a total space cadet"

"Like, gag me with a spoon!"

Part rock star, part satirist, part guitar hero, and part avant-garde composer, **Frank Zappa** had the only Top Forty hit of his career in 1982 with **"Valley Girl,"** which featured his four-teen-year-old daughter Moon Unit imitating the bizarre speech patterns of the rich, spoiled teenage girls from the San Fernando Valley. Zappa's biggest hit, however, came when he spoke out against censorship to a Senate subcommittee about the scourge of dirty rock lyrics. When asked how he could feel safe in a world where W.A.S.P. records weren't specifically labeled as being not for children, he replied, "I would say that a buzz saw blade be-tween the guy's legs on the album cover is a good indication that it's not for little Johnny."

Many thanks to our agent Todd Keithley of Jane Dystel Literary Management, who took an inchoate concept and turned it into a very fun project; Marcela Landres, our editor, who provided invaluable direction and perspective; Robert Kempe and Barbara Hauley, who helped with the research for this book; Jennifer Thornton, who did her very best to keep us from sounding illiterate; Sam "the man" Potts, who gave this book a mint design; and every songwriter and performer found within the preceding pages—thanks.

An extra special thanks to our righteous bosses, Bob Mecoy and Jeff Neuman, for putting up with invisible assistants for six weeks. And Sue Fleming-Holland, Mark Gompertz, David Greenberg, Dan Lane, Cherlynne Li, David Rosenthal, Trish Todd, Rebecca Webber, Jeff Wilson, and all the other folks at Simon & Schuster who made writing this book a pleasurable experience. The researchers at Photofest and Yvette Reyes at AP/Wide World helped enliven our text by providing the cool pictures found throughout the book. *The New Rolling Stone Encyclopedia of Rock & Roll* (the best music reference book in the universe), *Billboard Hot 100*

Acknowledgments

Charts: The Eighties, Lyrics.ch: The International Lyrics Server, and the IMDB (Internet Movie Database) made doing research relatively easy.

More thanks to Stephen Agovino, Andrea Au, Bob Baffert, Jerry Bailey, Carlene Bauer, Hal Bienstock, Hilary Black, Matt Blankman, Bosh, Trudy Brown, Joe Clancy, Jr., Sean Clancy, Jeff Colchamiro, Colony, Michael Conathan, Marian Courtney, Scott Cupolo, Dominique D'Anna, Kristi Delano, Doris Del Castillo, Janice Easton, Marie Florio, Paul Gillow, Tracy Alayne Hampel, Stephanie Hawkins, Kristie Holbrook, Jolene Howard, Neil Howard, Eric Huber, Casandra Jones, J. P. Jones, Kate Kaibni, Chris Lynch, Steve Malk, Kate Marlowe, Beth Marshall, Lindsay Mergens, Steve Messina, Richard Migliore, Mike at Park Slope Brewing Company, Blythe Miller, Chip Miller, Paul W. Morris, Keith O'Brien, Leo O'Brien, Laffit Pincay, Jr., Gregory Raskin, Irina Reyn, Denise Royal, Brant Rumble, Sam and Pedro at the Telephone Bar and Grill, Silver Charm, Alison Slagowitz, Mike Smith, Stacy Sparrow, Stan Stanski, Jennifer Stephenson, Christine Tanigawa, Ann Tappert, Susan Van Metre, John Velasquez, Robert "Penn" Warren, Paul Wasserman, Helen Watt, and Phil Yarnell, without whose help this book could not have been written.

And lastly, thanks to our families—God knows they deserve it!